POSTURE CONFIDENCE

"Everything You Need To Change Your Posture For Good"

By

Natalie A. Cordova, D.C.

Philip V. Cordova, D.C.

© Natalie A. Cordova | Philip V. Cordova

www.PostureConfidence.com

ISBN 978-0-9815607-0-0

POSTURE CONFIDENCE

"Everything You Need To Change Your Posture For Good"

Limits of Liability / Disclaimer of Warranty:

The authors and publisher of this book and the accompanying materials have used their best efforts in preparing this program. The authors and publisher make no representation of warranties with respect to the accuracy, applicability, fitness, or completeness of the contents of this program.

They disclaim any warranties (expressed or implied), merchantability, or fitness for any particular purpose. The authors and publisher shall in no event be held liable for any loss or other damages, including but not limited to special, incidental, consequential, or other damages. As always, the advice of a competent legal tax, accounting or other professional should be sought.

As always, before beginning any exercise or nutrition program, consultation and/or examination by a competent healthcare professional is recommended.

This manual contains material protected under International and Federal Copyright Laws and Treaties. Any unauthorized reprint or use of this material is prohibited.

Table of Contents

Introduction 1

Perfect Posture 9

Your Mattress 33

Your Chair 41

How Do You Get Bad Posture? 47

Nutrition To Help Your Posture 63

Posture Supports 69

Posture Problems That Can't Be Fixed 73

"Improve Your Posture" Practitioners 81

Posture Anatomy 89

Diagnose Your Posture Problem 119

Exercises 121

    General Posture Improvement 123

    Improving Neck & Shoulder Posture 149

Welcome to Posture Confidence!

This book contains everything you need to change your posture for good. If you take the time to review the information in this book, determine your needs, and then take action, you can <u>finally</u> correct your posture problem.

What difference would changing your posture make in your life? How would you feel about yourself when you're standing tall, looking your best and free of pain? While reading this book, you need to hold in your mind what you really hope to get out of it. A good, solid, motivating reason will make all the difference in the results you can expect.

In researching what is currently available to people seeking to improve their posture, We found a lot of general information and not a whole lot of specifics. You can get information about your spine and postural muscles, but what does that mean to you? How does it help?

You can get some good "tips" about changing your work station, but very little expert opinion on exactly what you need to do to change your already damaged posture. Then you mix in the advertisements from the makers of posture supports, chairs and mattresses and you can feel very confused. Some people begin to say, "*Just tell me what to do already!*"

Do you really care that your elbow should be at a certain angle? Are you going to measure? Do you just want exercises to make you look better? Are you getting ready to buy a chair or a bed so that your back finally stops hurting so much?

These are all wonderful reasons to begin exploring what you need to do to change your posture. However, it really goes beyond that. You have to understand that while some numbness and tingling in your hands may be an inconvenience, it is a significant symptom of a more serious problem. Your posture affects your health!

Because we've worked with patients with a multitude of neck, back and shoulder problems, we have a lot of experience in the effects of bad posture. We see younger patients with advanced degrees of spinal degeneration and elderly patients with the spines of someone half their age.

We have seen many spinal x-rays in which the age of the patient doesn't match what is on the film. Just as often as we see postural problems, disc problems, and degeneration of spinal joints in our elderly patients, the same conditions are present in people way too young to have these problems.

Less often, we see healthy and normal x-rays in patients that are advanced in age. (*In a way this makes sense that it's the people in pain that seek out chiropractic care. Not many patients that are already "pain-free" visit any type of health professional.*) The healthy spines aren't usually coming to see us, they're too busy out enjoying their good health!

This book is not meant to be just a narrative about how to make significant changes in your posture in the shortest amount of time possible, but as a reference guide for anything you are already experiencing. We want to be here to cheer you on and take notice that making a change in posture will make a change in your life.

Feel free to skip around to the sections that are most relevant to you. Getting ready to buy a new bed? Go straight to the section on choosing a mattress. However, if you are buying a new mattress thinking that it will end your back pain, you may need to make other changes first to see if your bed is really causing your problem.

If you think it's possible to end your pain prior to spending the money on the mattress, it is to your benefit to check out the rest of the book first. You still may need to change your mattress, but do it to support your now good posture.

There are a lot of benefits to achieving and obtaining good posture. Most of which will be very important to you long term, but a lot of benefits can be seen and felt immediately. You want to feel good about how you look, but we just want more for you than that.

It does you no good to look good and then deal with back pain. It also does no good to artificially reduce your back pain with medications while your spine continues to degenerate, waiting to cause even worse problems and pain for you in the future.

A few of the benefits that can be enjoyed immediately:

- Appear more confident
- Be taller
- Breathe easier
- Reduce stress
- Decrease pain

Some of the long-term benefits that you will enjoy later on:

- Avoid "The Hump" *or*
- Decrease the severity of your "hump"
- Maintain the health of your spinal discs
- Avoid complications of osteoporosis
- Avoid degenerative conditions of the spine

This book was created after years of answering questions from our patients and dealing with their concerns. We wanted our patients to have a resource to go to when they wanted posture information. In reviewing current materials, they seemed too technical, too general or just flat out not helpful.

This book is here to help you change your posture for good. Are you ready to enjoy better posture? Are you ready to be healthier?

Some of the exercises you will see may seem simple to you. Some people even say, *"Oh, I've seen that one."* That's great, but are you doing it?

The solution to your posture problem doesn't need to be complicated, it just needs to get done. Remember that it's your simple, uncomplicated daily activities and movements that got you into this position in the first place.

It's consistent and specific change that will make all the difference. We have no doubt that you can improve your posture. However, consistency is key

Let's get started!

"How does your posture form in the first place?"

HOW YOUR POSTURE FORMS

We'll get into more anatomy information a little later, but we want you to consider for a minute how your posture forms in the first place. Understand that your body was designed to work a specific way. So it makes sense that the curves in your spine were put there for a specific purpose.

First of all, your spine is supposed to have three curves. Your neck and low back curve the same way, something called a lordotic curve. Your mid back curves the other way (*although it may be curving too much in some people*), and this is called a kyphotic curve.

These are your normal curves, something you are supposed to have. Something you should strive to maintain.

However, when you are born, you only have one spinal curve. Your neck, mid back, and low back all have the kyphotic curve. This makes sense, if you can picture the fetal position. You are hunched up the same way inside your mother's womb.

You maintain this curve for some time and that's fine, because you're not doing a whole lot of activities that resist gravity. Basically, you're just being carried around. Your first "big moment" will be when you are finally able to hold up your head on your own.

This is where your neck curve, your first lordotic curve comes about.

What's the next step? Crawling.

Crawling serves to reinforce your neck and initiates the low back to curve. The next step is standing, and then walking. Here is where your full upright position and full gravity resistant activities will build your low back (*again, lordotic curve*). The curves all begin to stabilize as your body gains muscle control.

If the curves are all ultimately going to form based on you using your muscles and "teaching" your spine to stay a certain way, it makes sense that however you use your muscles will determine how the spine changes throughout your life.

The same muscles that created your posture in the first place will determine how good your posture will become and how well you'll be able to maintain your results.

PERFECT POSTURE

Posture is the result of the muscles tugging and pulling on your spine. If you work lots of muscles in the front of your body and not the back, you will have a hunched over body. If you strengthen your back muscles and not your front, you would be over extended.

To support the human skeleton, we are designed with quick fire muscles that are meant to contract, sustaining muscles that are more supportive and ligaments that allow for some movement but maintain the closeness of the bones.

The activities you do in the day will determine the strength, flexibility, and balance of your spine. If you have lots of diversity in your daily movements and you sit, stand, work out frequently and intensely for good posture, you probably have great posture.

If you sit or stand for long periods and don't work out then you probably have that hunched over posture. It would make sense that if you spend most of your day bent forward then you add in exercises that strengthen the front of your body you will have an even more hunched over posture.

There are a bunch of advertisements aimed at strengthening our abs. For the guys, the ads also include things to build up your chest because that's what we see when we look in the mirror. If we are going to exercise then we are guided to spend time on our *"show off"* muscles. The truth of the matters is that the more we hunch over the more we put our spine at risk for rapid degeneration and our spinal discs at risk for bulging and tearing.

When we are hunched over we look less confident and we scientifically take in less oxygen because our lung capacity is diminished which leads to less energy. Less energy leads to lots of problems!

Never mind the degeneration. We look sloppy bent over and we drag our feet in comparison with what we could have.

What would make sense? Strengthen the muscles that support your back from all angles. Bring balance to your body by finding your weak areas and strengthening them. Find tight and restricted areas and spend time loosening them and lengthening them.

It is important to have enough strength to sustain your posture all day long. The goal isn't to make everyone into a body builder, but to make the muscles strong enough to hold up your head and keep your shoulders back.

To sit at a computer for 5, 6 + hours at a time is a tough thing to do. If that's what you do, then you want to be able to support that. You don't want to find yourself five minutes into *"willing"* yourself into straight posture and then ending up hunched over when you stop focusing on it.

How do you make your muscles strong?

What muscles do you want to focus on strengthening?

Great questions! Targeting on the heavy hitters would be the rhomboids, latissmus dorsi, and paraspinals. The paraspinals are the muscles that parallel the spine. In the hunched over posture, these muscles are overstretched and weak. Strengthening will demand that they contract and thus start to retrain it to return to a shorter length over time.

"Perfect Posture" is within your reach if you take the time to counteract what you can't stop doing… your normal daily activities. In no way should you stop doing the things that you need to do to get through your day. Taking notice of how you do those things and keeping things balanced will go a long, long way.

SOME BASIC POSTURE TIPS...

The negative effects of poor posture take time to accumulate. Such everyday activities as sitting in your chair, looking at a computer, driving, standing, and sleeping are the main culprits in your posture habits and how your spine and overall health will be affected.

Poor posture becomes your habit, your nature, something that you just do. This second nature can cause painful symptoms due to the ongoing damage to spinal structures. Thankfully, your ability to change this bad habit is completely under your control.

The good news is that it doesn't take eight hours of exercise to counteract eight hours of bad posture. Positive results can happen with some changes to your habits and the addition of just a few minutes of exercise daily.

The following are some general tips to help you improve your posture and ergonomically reduce the strain on your spinal joints.

KNOW THE WARNING SIGNS

Back pain is often the first symptom that your spine is being affected by poor posture or poor ergonomics. Back pain that is worse after a long day of sitting in your office chair or standing for extended periods that improves after rest is a red flag for a posture related condition.

Neck pain that continues into the upper back or into the lower back is also an indicator. Pain that radiates into the arms or legs is a more serious indicator of an advancing condition and should not be ignored. However, should the symptoms alleviate or lessen after switching positions; posture deficiencies should certainly be evaluated.

Pain that begins following new activities that include extended sitting or standing or following the acquisition of a new chair, shoes, or workstation may also indicate a condition related to poor posture or poor mechanics. Pain that comes and goes for months is generally linked to postural strain and may be activity related.

GET UP AND MOVE

Not moving is more common in sitting-related jobs. Driving doesn't exactly involve a lot of movement. If you were to become engrossed in a computer project, you might move your fingers on the keyboard but not much else.

Not moving leads to muscle fatigue. As the muscles fatigue, it becomes easier for your body to revert to poor postural positions such as slouching and slumping. Maintaining these positions for extended periods puts additional pressure on the spine.

Movement is your key to reducing fatigue. Taking regular breaks (*like at least one per hour*) will return blood flow to the muscles and help keep them from getting tired. There are software programs out there, but a simple timer can help you remember to get up and move.

Regular exercise such as walking, swimming, or bicycling will help the body stay aerobically conditioned, while specific strengthening exercises will help the muscles surrounding the back to stay strong. These benefits of exercise promote good posture, which will, in turn, further help to condition muscles and prevent injury.

There are also specific exercises that will help maintain good posture. In particular, a balance of trunk strength with back muscles about 30% stronger than abdominal muscles is essential to help support the upper body and maintain good posture.

You can move while sitting by:

- Rolling your shoulders
- Stretching your neck
- Tapping your toes

You can move while standing by:

- Reaching overhead
- Exaggerate some deep breaths
- Stretching your arms behind you
- Tapping your toes

- Bending your knees
- Performing *"mini"* lunges

KEEP YOUR BODY STRAIGHT

Keep your body as straight as possible, particularly when sitting in your office chair or standing for extended periods. You may have evaluated this from side to side, but keeping your body weight distributed from front to back is also needed.

Walking, lifting heavy materials, holding a telephone, and typing are all moving activities that require attention to ergonomics and posture. It is important to maintain good posture even while moving to avoid injury. Back injuries are especially common while twisting and/or lifting and often occur because of awkward movement and control of the upper body weight alone.

USE POSTURE SUPPORTS WHEN NEEDED

Many people use posture supports as a posture *"fix."* Even though this is not the intended purpose of the posture support, it is not to say that supports and aids are not useful. (*Although, we often say that that we think they are overused and can be a crutch you simply don't need.*) Posture aids are particularly useful if the ergonomic chair or work area is not totally supportive of your spine as an individual.

It makes sense that even the best ergonomic chair cannot possibly properly accommodate everyone from 5' 0" to 6' 7". There has to be some may of helping the chair provide adequate support for everyone, even if it means adding stuff.

Footrests, portable lumbar back supports, or even a towel or small pillow can be used while sitting in an office chair and while driving. These are the types of posture supports you should consider.

Avoid regularly wearing high-heeled shoes, which can affect the body's center of gravity and change the alignment of the entire body, negatively affecting back support and posture.

When standing for long periods of time, placing a rubber mat on the floor can improve comfort. This will give your body more support and make it more likely that you will be able to maintain a healthy stance for a long period of time.

"What are the best ways to stand, sit, sleep..."

STANDING POSTURE

- Hold your head up straight with your chin in. Do not tilt your head forward, backward or sideways
- The bottoms of your ears should be in line with the middle of your shoulders
- Keep your shoulder blades back
- Keep your chest forward
- Keep your knees straight
- Tuck your stomach in. Do not tilt your pelvis forward or backward.

<u>If you need to stand for extended periods of time,</u>

- Adjust the height of the work table to a comfortable level
- Try to elevate one foot by resting it on a stool or box. After several minutes, switch your foot position.
- Make sure your shoes have good arch support

SITTING POSTURE

Many people think this is a silly thing to have to tell people. How hard is it to sit? Well, it must be very difficult because I hardly ever see anyone doing it right.

First of all, sit up! Your back should be straight with your shoulders back. Your butt should touch the back of your chair. (*Many people sit on the front of the chair's seat, totally eliminating the usefulness of the back of the chair.*)

Always think tall! Think of a string that goes through your spine and up through your head. Then picture someone pulling you up by this string.

Ever so gently, pull yourself up by this string. With your shoulders back, allow your chest to open up fully. Take in full breaths and think of the vitality and creativity that can come from better air flow to your body and your brain.

If absolutely necessary, use a back support (*even a small rolled up towel*) for your low back if the chair doesn't provide adequate support. Try to distribute your weight evenly between your hips.

Your knees should be bent at 90 degree angle. It's best if you can sit with your knees even or slightly lower than your hips. This takes a lot of strain off the hips. Do not cross your legs (*This alone keeps most people from having good sitting posture!*) and keep your feet flat on the floor.

One last thing... don't sit on your wallet! This can be difficult, but it's the equivalent of walking with one shoe on all day, or sitting on a block of wood in some cases. Either buy a smaller wallet and keep it in your front pocket, or keep you monster wallet and take it out when you sit (*including when driving*).

SLEEPING POSTURE

How to sleep is a common question our patients ask. It's amazing how many stomach sleepers are still out there! With all the strain we put on our necks all day, why do the same thing at night?

It's really not a good thing to sleep on your stomach. As a reformed stomach sleeper myself, I (*Dr. Philip*) understand your pain. (*Literally!*) Sleeping on my stomach led to a great deal of neck and low back pain before I was finally able to make the change.

The first problem with sleeping on your stomach has to do with your neck. Since your bed is most likely not outfitted with a slot for your nose to sit, you can either sleep face down and have trouble breathing or you can turn your head to one side.

Stomach sleepers are easy to identify by this one trait alone. You can likely turn your head very well to the side you turn to when you sleep, and about 50% to the other side. Already a problem.

Turning your head to one side does not in itself cause pain. Turning your head to one side while placing pressure on it for hours and hours every single night can lead to a problem.

The next problem is with your lower back.

When laying face down, the muscles of your thigh push up the lower aspect of your back forcing your lumbar spine into hyperflexion. That is, too much curve. The bones jam up on themselves and increase the likelihood of low back pain.

The same situation occurs in your lower back as it does in your neck. While laying face down for a moment doesn't cause a problem, laying in that position for hours will eventually lead to a low back problem and then pain.

Moving from being a stomach sleeper to a back sleeper is often a very difficult transition. Even if you start out on your back you probably won't stay that way. The next best way of sleeping is sleeping on your side.

To make the transition easier, you should invest in a body pillow. They are relatively inexpensive and can make a world of difference. In particular, you will want the body pillow (*or some kind of pillow*) to be between your knees. This alleviates a lot of pressure on your knees, hips, and low back.

"What about sleeping on my side?"

Sleeping on your side is the easiest transition to make if you are a chronic stomach sleeper. The change from sleeping on your stomach to sleeping on your back is often too drastic of change.

Throw in the fact that you are significantly more likely to start snoring when you are sleeping on your back and your partner may make the change even more difficult. (*It's often hard to become a back sleeper when you're getting poked and shoved all night.*)

The side sleeping position is my position of choice since becoming a reformed stomach sleeper.

To take the most pressure off your spine, there are just a couple of things to do. As always, I recommend involving a helper to take a look at your sleeping position. The most comfortable position is not always the best for you.

(*By the way, having a helper doesn't mean that you need someone to come over at bedtime and watch you sleep. Just lie down in your bed during the day, fully clothed, with the lights on and have them take a look.*)

Let's start with your pillow. Ideally, your head should remain straight, not dipping down or propped up due to too much of a pillow. It's almost always a bad idea to have more than one pillow (*unless they're paper thin*).

A pillow between your knees is also essential. Your hips and knees will thank you for taking the pressure off. I've seen pillows that strap onto your leg, which keeps them from getting "*lost*" in the middle of the night. This isn't the most attractive thing I've ever seen and I always wondered what would happen in case of a fire. Here I am running from my home with a pillow strapped to my leg...

The best solution for this is the body pillow. It gives you something to grab onto and mimics some of the things you probably liked about sleeping on your stomach and allows a pillow to be between your knees. Since you are holding it, it will move with you should you roll over.

The idea is to limit any rotation of your pelvis and, therefore, your lumbar spine. Have the pillow firmly against your body, with your top leg on the pillow with your ankle and foot supported on it too.

Your upper body should have the top arm wrapped around the pillow so that there's no rotation of the upper back.

The only drawback to the body pillow is that it's so big! It can be like adding an additional person in the bed. The trade off is well worth it and many stores sell these giant pillows, so they are easy to find for under $10.

So, what is the best way to sleep?

So you've finally decided to sleep on your back? Good for you... as long as you don't snore... or even if you do and you sleep by yourself. Sleeping on your back should be the easiest way to keep your spine in good alignment for the six to eight hours each night.

I know sleeping sounds simple. Lay on your back. Go to sleep. Wake up. What else is there?... A lot!

Let's keep in mind that we want to keep your spine in the best position possible when you sleep. If nothing else, this should keep you from continuing to damage your spine each night even if it's not necessarily fixing anything.

If you were standing with good posture, you would want your head over your shoulders. Not behind your shoulders (*less of an issue when you're standing*) and not in front of your shoulders. This is all about your pillow. Your pillow should not make your chin tuck forward.

Again, we're going to need a helper. Lay on your bed and have someone take a look. Does it look like your head is falling backwards? Does it appear that your head is higher than your chest? Adjust the height of your pillow (*or pillows*) until you appear pretty straight.

If you want to be aggressive you can even get a small hand towel (*not a bath or beach towel*), roll it up, put some rubber bands around it and put it under your neck. This will support your neck's normal curve.

There are specialty pillows that accomplish the same thing, but the towel is free! Finally, put a pillow under your knees. This has been shown to take the most pressure off your low back and is really comfortable. The key here is that your legs should be slightly bent without you trying to keep them bent. Let the pillow do the work.

The reason for this is that many of us have very tight hip flexor muscles that don't relax when we sleep. If we keep our legs straight, then the hip flexors (*being attached to the spine*) will make our spine draw up, pinching our discs and nerves. As you improve the flexibility of your hip flexors, you may be able to wean yourself from the pillow under the legs.

DRIVING POSTURE

- Use a back support (*lumbar roll*) at the curve of your back. You can use a posture support or use a small towel with rubber bands around it to keep it in place.

- Your knees should be at the same level or higher than your hips. If the knees are higher than the hips, the angle between the spine and the thighs reduces. This begins to increase stress on your lower back.

- Move the seat close to the steering wheel to support the curve of your back (*without being so close that you are worried about what would happen if the airbag were to deploy*). The seat should be close enough to allow your knees to bend and your feet to reach the pedals

- Your elbows should be in a relaxed bend, about 20 degrees. Your upper back, shoulders, and neck should be relaxed. You should be able to take in deep breaths and calmly focus on your driving.

"What about my posture when I use my computer?"

COMPUTER POSTURE

Dealing with your proper computer posture is something I am asked all the time. There are plenty of diagrams, workstations, and chairs touting that they are the answer to your computer posture issues.

Your computer posture should be an extension of the exercises you are already doing to improve your posture. Worse case scenario, your computer posture should not be taking away from the good work you're doing on improving your posture.

SITTING IN YOUR CHAIR

Place your feet firmly on the floor.

Your feet should be flat on the floor, providing the necessary support. If your feet cannot make it to the floor, adjusting your chair or adding a footrest will help you get the support you need.

Your chair should support your thighs.

Your thighs should be parallel to the floor, but they can be angled downwards slightly as long as they are being supported by your chair. The key is that you don't want your thighs angled up. This will tilt your pelvis and back, causing your spine to also roll back. Aim to have you're the pelvis upright.

Your chair should support your upper back.

Your shoulders should be able to relax, allowing your arms to hang loosely.

Your arms should be horizontal.

Especially when typing, your elbows should be bent at 90 degrees and your forearms should be parallel to the floor. If this is not the case, your desk or your chair may not be at the right height. Your keyboard should also be in front of you, and your arms should be able to rest comfortably on the armrests.

Your chair should be adjustable.

In the home office, it is not uncommon that a dining room chair is being used as a desk chair. I know it is possible that the chair is exactly the right height, but not likely. An adjustable chair makes it possible for you to make the necessary changes to bring your body to the right position.

Your armrests should be padded and adjustable.

Make sure your armrests are not too high; you should be able to relax your shoulders and let your arms naturally *"fall"* to the correct position. It defeats the purpose of having *"armrests"* if you have to use work or effort to get your arms on them. This makes your shoulders hunch. Padded armrests also have some *"give"* to allow easier movements while working.

Your chair should be able to rotate.

If your chair can rotate, that means you don't have to. Make sense? You can still sit straight. It's even better if your chair also has wheels, allowing you to roll into any position or location in your workspace.

KEYBOARD AND MOUSE

Your mouse and keyboard should be at the same height.

Keeping your mouse and keyboard at the same height and preferably near each other will minimize the posture changes each time you switch from one to the other.

Your wrists should be straight.

Keeping your wrists straight (*neutral*) reduces the risk of repetitive stress (*strain*) injury (*RSI*). If your wrists are forced to bend up, down, or to any side while you use your keyboard and mouse, you are increasing the likelihood that you will develop wrist problems, including carpal tunnel syndrome.

Your keyboard should be at the same height as your elbows.

This will keep your forearms level and your wrists neutral. It also means that you cannot keep your keyboard on top of your desk! Keyboard trays can be easily installed to bring your keyboard down to a non-damaging level.

You should be able to reach all the keys without straining.

This may be getting a little picky, but you should be able to easily reach all the keys of your keyboard. Everyone is not the same size! Thankfully, there are now smaller keyboards available to help with this. This is just one more thing to consider when looking for every possible way to keep yourself from developing problems from your everyday activities.

Remember, it's sometimes the smallest things that lead to some of the biggest problems when that small thing is repeated over and over and over again.

MONITOR

Your monitor should be directly in front of you.

Okay, pretty obvious right? Nope. I still have to tell my patients to do this. You should not have to turn your neck to look at your monitor while typing. You should strive to get everything as straight as possible.

Your eyes should be about 2 feet from the monitor.

If your monitor is very large, you may have to move back a little more. This again seems like an easy one but, with the invention of the wireless keyboard, people are zooming all over the place in their chairs and keeping their monitors in strange places.

Your eyes should be level with the top of the monitor.

Ideally, you should be able to look slightly down to see the middle of the screen. You should not have to lean your head back or forward to see your monitor. If your monitor height is adjustable, this should be an easy step for you. If not, you can use a book or other handy object to get your monitor to a good level.

It's better to have the monitor too high than too low. (Although we're not recommending putting your monitor on the ceiling!) Still, it's better to be looking slightly up instead of looking down.

YOUR LAPTOP

I don't think there's a perfect way to use your laptop. You've going to have to sacrifice something. If you actually put the laptop on your lap while sitting in a chair, you're probably slumping.

Put the laptop on top of your desk, and you're probably sacrificing your wrists, but you can save your neck and back.

Ideally (*and I haven't seen this much*), you sit at a table that is low enough to support your wrists being straight. You sit up straight, and you move the screen so that you can look slightly down on it.

"How do I go about choosing the right mattress & office chair?"

YOUR MATTRESS

A common scenario in our office is a new patient that arrives complaining of low back pain. *What have you done about it so far?* I ask. *"Well, the first thing I did was go out and buy the best mattress I could. I figured it was because my bed wasn't right."*

While this is not an illogical conclusion, my next question seems to floor them. *How did you know you were getting the right mattress for you?* *"I, uh, bought the best one!"* Just about every mattress company has different versions of their mattresses. They aren't selling the *"This will hurt your back"* model vs. the *"This won't hurt your back"* model.

Some of the lower priced mattress options may be just right for some people. How do you decide? It seems there is a lot of confusion out there. You are not the only one.

If the average person spends one-third of their life in bed (*approximately*), you would be surprised to find out there has been little scientific research performed on mattresses.

THE FOUNDATION

We'll get to the mattress portion in a minute, but let's quickly review the foundation of your bed also known as the box spring. The box spring supports the mattress and is comparable to shocks in your car.

Many people ignore the benefits of a box spring and either eliminate it from their set up or they take their good mattress and put it on the floor. The foundation can have springs (*that's why they call it a box spring*) or no springs.

The springs allow your weight to be more evenly distributed across its frame for better wear and tear. The benefit of the weight distribution can be outweighed by the possibility that your box spring will "*squeak.*"

Foam mattresses typically utilize a wooden frame, as springs are not needed. Foam foundations are available for the foam mattresses and should not be used on coiled spring mattresses. There are different grades of wood that do not necessarily affect your ability to sleep, but have a determination on their lifespan. Obviously cheaper wood will wear faster and will begin to lose their supportive effect sooner.

Mixing and matching your mattress and foundations is not recommended. This can lead to incomplete support and it's not worth reducing the effectiveness of your investment. Also, the mixing and matching (*particularly if you are putting a new mattress on an old box spring*), may void your warranty.

A quality mattress should last you between eight and ten years. Combine that with your comfort and desire to avoid back problems, and you've got quite a decision on your hands. We will provide with you an outline choosing a bed, but if you follow all of these suggestions and still aren't comfortable with the bed please don't continue to use it!

Your doctor can offer some suggestions (*or things to avoid*) if you have a specific condition. Also, if you find that you have a very similar body type as a family member and they are thrilled with their bed, you have another leg up on making your decision. Even if they didn't like a particular bed this added information can be very helpful.

BUYING NEW

Considering even the best mattress should likely be replaced every ten years, how much available use are you getting by purchasing a used bed? Probably not a whole lot. The mattress may look fine, but the core of the mattress is probably ready for a change. After all, why were they getting rid of it?

Another issue may be the likelihood of dust mites or other pests. The old mattress may not meet updated safety standards. Remember, you will be spending one-third of your life on this thing. Buying new is almost surely the right place to start.

DETERMINE THE SIZE

If we had to summarize this section in one sentence, it would be *"bigger is better."* Keep in mind that your bed will need to fit in your bedroom. Other than that, get the biggest bed you can afford. Any extra room you can get will help the comfort of you and/or your partner.

This part may seem obvious, but it is often overlooked... try out the bed. If you and your partner will be sleeping on the bed each night, go to the store together and try it out! Some people get caught up in thinking they can't simulate their sleep environment, so they don't think about trying out beds in public or during the day.

The more things you can rule out instead of leaving them to chance, the more likely your success in choosing your bed.

MATTRESS FIRMNESS

We have heard people say for years that when they had issues with their mattress or their back, that they went out and bought the *"firmest"* mattress they could buy. *"I bought the best mattress I could get, it's so firm!"* The results were always mixed.

Some people would be happy they got the firm mattress, others had to return it. There wasn't a lot of research. Firm mattresses have been prescribed for years by every medical professional (*but not chiropractors*). The underlying philosophy being that the while the soft mattress feels good, it doesn't provide much support. How to know for sure?

Now we have available beds that can adjust the firmness, so that you can vary the result between you and your partner. (*See more information under "Air Mattresses" later in this chapter.*) Still, are you getting the best support? Finally more research has become available.

A research study out of Spain using 313 patients with a history of low back pain and gave them firm and medium-firm mattresses. All of the participants had previously complained of feeling pain in their lower backs when lying in bed and when they were getting out of bed. The participants were not told which bed they were using. The group with the medium-firm mattresses reported improvements in their low back pain twice as often as those on the firm mattresses.

Some believe the study may be a bit skewed by the idea that the patients included simply needed a new mattress. Many people don't change their mattresses periodically or purchase a used mattress that has already passed its usefulness period.

Still, would you be the person that reported improvement with the firm mattress? There are just a handful of studies that report improvements with a firm mattress, but since there is overall little research it is difficult to determine. Also, research can often only provide the information for categories like *"more likely"* or *"twice as likely"* but rarely do we get anything that says *"always."*

I have learned in practice that there are therapies that work best for most people, but rarely is there anything that works across the board with every patient with every condition. Much of this is trial and error, starting with the most logical conclusion and moving on from there.

Let's help you get to your most logical conclusion, but realize you are going to have to try out the mattresses until you arrive at the right conclusion for you. As such, it's usually best to find a store with a liberal policy on trying out the bed. We recommend never purchasing a bed that won't let you use it for at least a thirty-day trial period (*Most will allow longer*).

Surveys have indicated that orthopedic doctors continue to recommend firm mattresses to their patients anywhere from 2 out of 3 to as much as 3 out of 4 times. Chiropractors have long recommended that this may not be the right choice.

Chiropractors have traditionally recommended a medium-firm mattress with the addition of a 1 ½" to 2" thick padding. The philosophy behind this is that the extra padding allows a more evenly disbursed support to better adapt to the normal curvatures (*there's 3*) of the spine.

The additional padding is usually available where you buy your mattress and other stores that sell bedding supplies.

COILED SPRING MATTRESS

The coiled spring mattress is the most common type on the market today, and the type that most people have become accustomed. There are two types; continuous and independent.

In a continuous spring mattress, each coil is an ongoing part of one system. This does have the negative effect that you can't jump on one side without spilling a glass of wine on the other side(*per a popular commercial*). The advantage of this type of system is that it makes the mattress less likely to begin sagging in one place. The disadvantage is that the system cannot be responsive to the individual shape of your body.

Independent coil mattress systems (*as the name suggests*) utilize coils that are separate to give more flexible support across the individual sections of your body. While these systems are more expensive, those that opt for a cheap version can be disappointed when the coils give way quickly. Since more stress can be put on an individual coil, there may be uneven wear and tear.

The total number of coils is also typically indicative of the quality of the mattress. However, there is no amount of coils that has been determined to be the best. The more coils, the more firm the mattress.

As we've discussed, if the mattress is too firm it may not be the most ideal mattress for you. If the mattress has few coils (*more common in cheaper mattresses*) it will be less firm, but it will also put more strain on the coils.

AIR MATTRESS

We're not recommending inflating a raft used in your swimming pool and sleeping on that. Even the inflatable beds used for your unfortunate guests are not likely going to provide the right kind of support (*as evidenced by your back soreness on your last visit to the in-laws*).

We're talking about the mattresses that use inflatable air chambers to adjust firmness with a remote control. For example, Select Comfort assigns you a number based on a *"pressure mapping"* system that uses a computer to determine which level of firmness is best for you.

Also good for couples, the beds have two separate chambers so that your partner can have an entirely different number than you. This is particularly useful if you need a firm mattress while your partner needs something totally different.

The complaints we've heard from dissatisfied customers (*we've heard mostly good things*) is that the bed is not as comfortable as they would like. In particular, the air chamber is surrounded by padding and it's possible to roll off the air chamber portion and into the edging. This issue seems to be more prevalent in the lower end models.

We tried an air mattress with a pillow top and were unable to find the air chamber or the hard edge mentioned by others.

FOAM MATTRESS

Originally developed by NASA to help astronauts deal with the enormous G forces experienced during takeoff, the material has now been put in use in our mattresses. The idea being that if the foam can absorb the forces of gravity during takeoff, surely it can help support you during sleep.

The *"memory"* foam absorbs your body heat and molds itself to the contours of your body to support as needed. The foam is also beneficial for couples, as it adapts individually. This can be particularly useful if one partner is significantly larger than the other.

One drawback I've heard is that if you tend to *"get hot"* while you sleep, the material is more likely to exaggerate your body heat rather than help dissipate it. In other words, if you get hot sleeping in a spring mattress, expect that you'll get hotter sleeping in the foam mattress.

If this is not a concern for you (*maybe you're always cold*), then this mattress may be the right choice for you. These mattresses are typically not cheap, but they are certainly catching on. They are gaining support from medical experts and chiropractors who are pleased with the spinal support offered. The foam allows your hips and shoulders to sink into the bed while supporting your waist and legs.

There is yet to be any truly significant research to support any of these claims, but it does seem to make sense from a logic standpoint. People that own these types of beds say that the mattress takes some adjustment time since they don't feel as plush as what they may be used to.

"*Mattress experts*" recommend that your memory foam mattress include a minimum of 4 to 5 cm of foam in order to properly provide the support you are seeking. If you can't afford a memory foam mattress or want to upgrade your current mattress, you may consider adding a foam mattress topper.

HOW OFTEN TO GET A NEW MATTRESS

The short answer is every ten years. However, this is based on you following the suggestions of the manufacturer (*which most people don't do*). Most mattresses include warranties from ten to fifteen years, but that's for the mattress not your level of support or comfort.

It is typically recommended by the mattress manufacturers that your mattress be rotated at least twice per year, but every three months is best. The goal is to reduce or eliminate creating any sagging or indentations in your sleeping area. If you start sinking into the bed, this can lead to back problems.

SUMMARY

Overall, you're going to want a mattress that's not too hard and not too soft. One that is right for you. This may seem that I'm dancing around the subject, but every body is not made equally. I have relatives that happily sleep on the floor to help their back, something that would leave me incapacitated for days.

Think about what you want this mattress to do. You want support on all of your key spinal areas while gravity does its thing on you while you're asleep. If your mattress were super-firm (*like made out of metal*), it would have no "*give*" to it and your shoulder would be compressed and bear the entire force while you slept on your side.

If your bed were super-soft, while laying on your side your shoulders and hips would bear the entire pressure. However, your body would have the support it needs from below and points on your spine that are unsupported would begin to sag. The sagging every night would put extra stress on your spine, pulling it out of alignment and stressing the ligaments and joints of the spine.

The ideal scenario would be to find a mattress that conforms to your pressure points while providing adequate support to the natural curves of your spine. Finding this ideal scenario is not going to happen without some trial and error. That's why we recommend working with a local store (*if possible*) that offers a liberal return policy if you're not happy or if it's just not the right bed for you.

I will recommend, however, that you steer clear of the spring mattresses. Their time has come and gone and there are just better alternatives available. The air bed people that assign you a number have a great device that "*pressure maps*" where you are putting your weight when you lay down and then assign the right firmness for you.

I think for most people, the foam mattress is going to give great support for their posture issues. Other than getting warm, the responses I've heard from patients seem to give this the best chance for your success.

YOUR CHAIR

If you're reading this section first, you know that your chair is not the right one for you. Your neck hurts or your back hurts. Before you go out and spend a lot of money on the top of the line chair, double-check your workstation and make sure that you've covered all the bases there.

Saying your chair can make or break your posture is not totally true. I am still going to reinforce that you must exercise to have good posture. Getting a chair to fix your posture will only lead to frustration. Your chair should support your good posture and help you maintain what you've worked on.

Still, too many people think that they can passively improve their posture and that is just not true! Select your chair with the idea that you will be diligently working on improving your posture through exercise and then you will steadily improve your surroundings to support your efforts.

We are not all the same height and weight, nor do we all sit at the same workstation for the same lengths of time. This is why I can't just say, "*Go buy Chair A and good posture to you!*" That would be nice. Knowing what you're looking for and what to avoid combined with your budget will help you get the most out of your selection.

Here are the most important things to consider:

- Chair must be height adjustable
- Armrests must be height adjustable
- With your buttocks against the back of the chair, attempt to pass a clenched fist between the front of your chair and the back of your calf. If you can't do that, the chair is too deep for you.
- If the chair is too deep, you can try to adjust the backrest of the chair forward or insert a lumbar support.
- Backrest of chair must be adjustable
- Chair should offer lumbar support (*low back support*)
- The chair's material should breathe (*cloth instead of a hard surface*)
- The chair should swivel (*rotate*)
- The chair should have a rounded front edge (*allows for better circulation*)

Of course the biggest, most innovative (*at least it was when it came out in 1994*) and famous ergonomic chair is the Aeron office chair. It has won more awards than any other office chair in history and has revolutionized the way manufacturers approach ergonomic design.

The Aeron is adjustable for lumbar depth, lumbar height, tilt tension, seat-pan angle, seat height, armrest angle and armrest height. It comes in three sizes, so it's adaptable for very short or very tall people.

The seat material is Pellicle mesh rather than fabric, and the chair comes with a 12-year warranty. However, not everyone finds this chair comfortable so it's not the absolute best choice for everyone.

The primary complaint against this chair is that it doesn't adapt well to the many positions in which you might like to sit. It's designed for sitting properly at your desk, not leaning back or putting your legs in various positions.

SUMMARY

Just like in choosing your mattress, you're going to have to check out the chairs. There's still a lot you can rule out sitting in the store, though. Many people read a guide and say, *"My chair has to fit this way and that way..."* but they forget that they don't really use their chair that way.

You have to consider what you do during your day. Are you primarily on your keyboard or your mouse? Do you have a large workspace to cover? (*This can make a difference in the type of wheels or casters you choose.*)

Do you lean back in your chair a lot? How much space is available for you to fit this super-chair you're going to buy? Are you accepting the recommendation of someone half your size? Or twice your size?

"How did I get bad posture in the first place?"

HOW DO YOU GET BAD POSTURE?

Posture starts out as a bad habit. Something you begin doing as a result of your normal daily activities. I can't imagine anyone starts out wishing that their shoulders roll forward, or their head juts out. Your posture problem may have started with a lack of confidence. You just started hanging your head down.

I see teenagers slumping as just a part of being a teenager. I see tall kids slouching to appear more similar in height to their peers and teenage girls folding their arms and slouching forward as a way to hide their growing chests.

Whether it starts out as a lack of confidence or a way to fit in, this may have started you down the path to bad posture.

If you happen to survive with good posture into your adult years, your chosen job or occupation may begin to wear you down. Take a look at your typical daily activities. You do almost the same things every single day. You may be working on different projects, but you still just sit in front of the computer all day, or at least in the same position all day.

Maybe your workstation is set up for a 5' 0" person, but you're 5' 10" and you are straining to fit into your confined surroundings. Your chair may be top of the line, but not suitable for someone with your back condition or routine.

Maybe your normal daily activities includes going home and plopping down into a comfortable but non-supportive couch every night and holding that position until your four to six hours of favorite shows run their course.

Here's a way of understanding more easily what we're talking about. Let's say you go to the gym and only do dumbbell curls to build up your biceps. That's it. Day after day, week after week you only work on your biceps. Would your biceps build up?

Sure they would! The opposing muscle that creates balance in your upper arm is the triceps. Would your triceps build up? Of course not. You may get some residual benefits from lifting or carrying the weight around, but you will be creating a very unbalanced upper arm.

It's only a matter of time in this scenario before the muscle that is worked out becomes stronger and shorter while your triceps because longer and weaker. Eventually something's going to give.

To avoid this problem, all you would have to have done was work the opposing muscle to counteract the muscle that is being worked all the time. How much more? That depends on the results you were experiencing. It's entirely possible that you would need to work your triceps twice as often as your biceps to get good results.

You still have to watch and look for balance. Posture is no different. If you are driving to work each day, sitting at a computer all day, then driving home and then sitting on the couch all of your activities are being done in front of you. There is virtually no time during the above example that you give your back muscles any opportunity to work or grow stronger

What's going to happen? Your front muscles will become shorter and stronger while your back muscles will become longer and weaker. And so the path to bad posture begins…

Before I show you how to fix your posture problem, I really want you to understand some of the negative effects of bad posture. If you are going to make any type of significant and lasting change, you need to have more motivation than just "*I want to look better.*"

Looking better is a good goal and something absolutely attainable by doing the exercises in this book. However, we need all the motivation we can get to keep you working on areas of imbalances for the rest of your life.

There's a lot going on with bad posture and it's time you find out.

WHAT ARE THE EFFECTS OF BAD POSTURE?

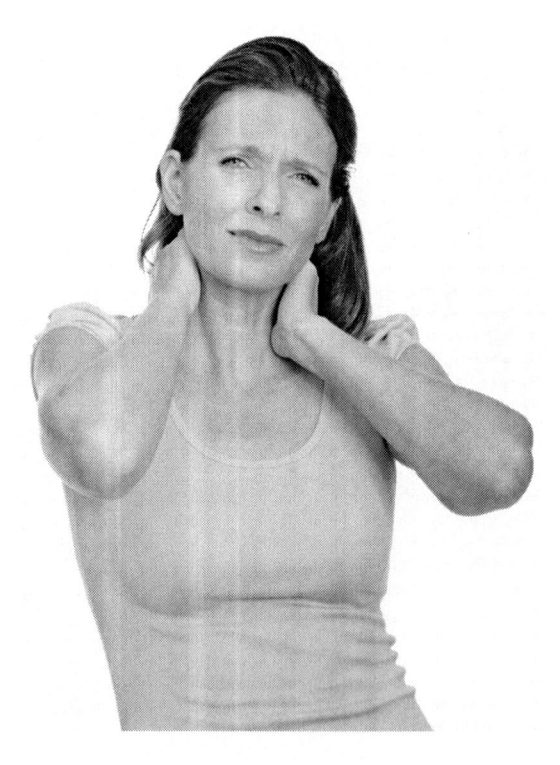

Without exaggeration, bad posture is one of the leading causes of poor health. While we're including neck and back pain, there's a lot more to it. Your body is designed to work a specific way. You have two ears, two arms and two legs. In general, your body should be pretty balanced from side to side, front and back.

When your spine and body are in their best alignment, your body has its best chance to work and function in a healthy and pain-free way. Each degree of movement in the wrong direction may not cause pain or health problems, but it certainly increases the likelihood that the problems will occur.

Depending on where you look and who you ask, bad posture can be the initial cause of any and all of the following health problems;

- Arthritis
- Back Pain
- Carpal Tunnel Syndrome
- Chest Pain
- Degenerative Joint Disease (DJD)
- Digestive Problems
- Eye Strain
- Herniated Discs
- Hormone Imbalances
- Fatigue
- Headaches
- Joint Pain
- Muscle Strain
- Neck Pain
- Pain Between The Shoulder Blades
- Respiratory Problems
- Repetitive Stress Injury (RSI)
- Rotator Cuff Injury
- Sciatica
- Urinary/Incontinence problems

However, we can go our whole life without realizing that any of the above problems are due to our poor posture. You can take an aspirin for your headache or any other pain reliever for your back pain, maybe even visit your doctor, get injections, or even surgery!

Take a look at how drug companies currently spend their advertising dollars. Do they say anything about solving the cause of the problem? No. They strictly talk with you about your symptoms and the new anti-symptom chemical that has been developed. If you cough, you get a cough-suppressant without mention of why your body thinks it's a good idea to cough.

Your doctor may run you through many treatments and tests determining what you have, but may not address how you got that way in the first place or what you can do to keep the problem from coming back.

All for something that could have been prevented with less than ten minutes per day of exercise and changing some of our surroundings so that our normal daily activities can be performed with proper movement.

Working on your posture is a way to look to the *cause* of your problem, rather than just the symptom. The negative effects described above were caused by something, and it just may be your posture.

Here's the science behind one of the negative effects of "posture syndromes" (*like head forward posture and rounded shoulders*).

It has been determined that an average head weighs eight to ten pounds. (*Let's use ten pounds for the rest of this example.*) If your head is in its proper alignment over your shoulders, your spine is able to act like a big shock absorber as it was designed, minimizing the strain and evenly distributing the ten pounds of weight.

Gravity is always pulling on your head regardless of its position over your shoulders. However, with your head over your shoulders, the load on your spine is just ten pounds. For every inch your head moves forward, the effective load on your spine increases by a factor of ten. **Ten!** A ten-pound head one inch in front of the shoulders is like having a 20-pound head.

Move your head forward another inch? Now your head is creating 30 pounds of stress and strain on the muscles of your neck and back. After all, they are the muscles holding everything up and they will bear the strain of the increase in weight.

Okay, so what. Your neck thinks your head is heavy. How does this effect you long term? When the load or pressure to your spine is increased, the bones will change to accommodate the increased amounts. Typically, the bones will remodel with the increase of osteophytes, also known as bone spurs. Yikes! You definitely don't want these if you can help it.

Was it really that subtle, or did you get a lot of warning signs along the way? That 30-pound head creates knots in your shoulder muscles. Then those 2 or 3 knots begin to make the entire neck and shoulder area tense and tight. Sound like anyone you know?

Meanwhile, the bones underneath are slowly but steadily creating the bones spurs to effectively shut down the area or joint that is not functioning correctly or that is just unable to support the activities on its own.

Your body gives you warning signs. We tend to tune them out, but please don't do that. Recognize what your body is trying to tell you.

Some studies indicate that some bad posture can alter the amount of blood flow to the spinal cord. Some positions have been known to cause disc damage. Poor postural mechanics affect your rib cage, stopping your ability to take in all the oxygen you might need in order to take a full breath.

That's a lot of stuff that can happen with bad posture, wouldn't you agree? Next I'm going to cover in a bit more detail some of the devastating effects of bad posture, conditions I see in my practice everyday.

DEGENERATIVE JOINT DISEASE

Since we are chiropractors, this is an area of particular interest for us. We see degenerative joint disease (DJD) in most of our patients. It's interesting how quickly patients dismiss it when they see it on their x-rays. *"Oh, that's common for someone my age, right?"*

Maybe, but *"common"* and *"normal"* are two different things.

It is quite *"common"* for me to see an area of spinal degeneration at the same spinal level as where the patient is having their complaint! That means you say *"I have pain right here"* and we end up showing you an x-ray that the spine has degeneration at that very spinal joint. A direct correlation.

The interesting thing about this is that DJD is not a painful process. You can go from totally normal to degenerating and then on to spinal fusion with no symptoms at all! Let me say it again. You can have a vertebra with a problem, have bone spurs form and your spinal joint fuse… all with no pain whatsoever.

Degenerative joint disease is evidence of a long term spinal problem. DJD does not form overnight, it takes years. Effectively, your spine has to function poorly and continue to function poorly for a long time in order for DJD to show up on your x-rays.

"*But my pain just started last week.*" We certainly believe our patients when they tell us this, but it doesn't change the fact that while the symptoms started last week, the problem began some time ago. Changes that are visible on x-ray just don't show up that quickly.

It may very well happen that those people sitting in front of the computer all day will one day wake up so pain so bad they have to get that bone spur surgically removed!

DJD is known as a "*wear and tear*" condition. A similar example would be driving around with your wheels out of alignment. The evidence is not in your wheels, but in your tires. You can look to uneven tire wear as proof that your wheels are out of alignment. You can replace your tires attempting to fix your problem, but your tires will just wear out quickly again until you address the wheel alignment. You can't replace your spine, you have to get it in alignment.

In addition, the process of DJD starts with wearing out of the joint's surface, followed by bone spurs, narrowing of the joint space, hardening of the bone at the joint surface and deformity of the joint.

DJD is also known as osteoarthritis, OA, and osteoarthrosis. Symptoms include joint stiffness, pain, and limitation in the joint's normal range of motion. (*Like your neck turns very well to the left, but not the right.*)

This doesn't have to happen to you. Keep reading and we'll get to the part where you can do something about this soon enough.

Another negative effect of bad posture is the herniated disc.

HERNIATED DISCS

Your spinal discs are rubbery pads found between your vertebrae. The inner portion of the disc is filled with a jelly-like substance, while the outer ring is more cartilage-like. An injury or problem with these discs is sometimes referred to as the disc having "*slipped*" or "*ruptured.*" Herniated discs are a common reason why someone visits a chiropractor.

The discs act as shock absorbers in your spine. When the spine is in its best alignment, the amount of stress on the disc is evenly distributed across the entire disc. When the spine moves out of alignment, increased stress and pressure are placed on some portions of the disc.

Since the disc is filled with a jelly-like substance, as increase pressure is place on one side of it, the jelly will eventually have to go somewhere. A disc is said to have herniated when the center jelly pushes through the outer edge of the disc. This can create pressure in the center, affecting the spinal cord or towards the side and create pressure on spinal nerves.

The spinal nerves are very sensitive to pressure, inevitably leading to pain, numbness, or weakness. In addition to bad posture, there are other activities that can weaken the disc. Still, most of the following activities create extra pressure on the disc due to starting the activity with improper posture.

The activities include:

- Improper lifting
- Excessive body weight
- Physical trauma

Symptoms of a herniated disc include:

- Pain
- Weakness in one extremity (*arm or leg*)
- Numbness or tingling (*a "pins-and-needles" sensation*) in one extremity
- Loss of bowel or bladder control (*This is considered an emergency situation, get to a hospital!*)
- Burning pain
- Pain increases with flexed movements, like bending forward or looking down
- Increased pain when bearing down, like when using the restroom

Not all neck and back pain is the result of a herniated disc. You can also have numbness and tingling for other reasons. Diagnosing a herniated disc cannot be done on your own. Your health professional will likely need x-rays and/or MRI examination to arrive at the best diagnosis. While the doctor will be able to tell whether or not the disc is involved without the extra tests, the tests will pinpoint where the disc is involved and how severe.

Treatment for this injury includes chiropractic adjustments, therapy, steroid injections and surgery. More information on treatment for herniated disc is found in the section under "Posture Problems That Can't Be Fixed."

ROTATOR CUFF INJURY

Your *"rotator cuff"* refers to the muscles and tendons that make up your shoulder joint. There are four major muscles; the subscapularis, the supraspinatus, the infraspinatus, and the teres minor. (*You don't have to remember all of these, but they are sometimes referred to as your SITS muscles.*)

The tendons of these muscles connect to your humerus (*the bone of your upper arm*) and your scapula (*shoulder blade*). They help move and rotate your shoulder, but they also help hold it in place.

Your shoulder is the most mobile joint in your entire body, capable of moving in nearly every direction. The increased mobility causes a decrease in stability. This means that if you are using your shoulder in just a couple of its movements all the time, the other muscles can become weak. This will make the shoulder even more unstable.

Can you really hurt your shoulder with bad posture? Absolutely. I have had patients with non-active lifestyles come in with rotator cuff tears. No trauma, at least not that they were aware of. That is, they couldn't remember or tell me about any time in which they *"pulled"* their shoulder or fell down or anything like that.

Instead, the trauma was their bad posture. Of their four rotator cuff muscles, one or more (*usually the supraspinatus*) was not getting the strengthening it needed, while it was being stretched and strained repeatedly with shoulders that were rolling forward.

Gravity kept pulling and pulling on the shoulder joint until, finally, something had to give. That *"give"* occurred in the form of a tear and pain was the result.

More commonly, rotator cuff injuries are the result of falling, lifting, and repetitive arm movement (*especially those movements that are done overhead*). In other words, having bad posture for years is the equivalent of suffering a bad fall. Interesting.

Signs and symptoms that you may have a rotator cuff injury:

- Pain and tenderness in your shoulder joint
- Painful shoulder movements; especially reaching overhead, reaching behind your back, lifting and pulling.
- Pain when you sleep on that shoulder
- Shoulder weakness
- Decrease in your shoulder's range of motion
- The tendency to avoid doing things with your shoulder

You may not even recognize that you have limited range of motion in your shoulder. Take this simple test: Can you scratch all areas of your own back? Are there large sections that you simply can't reach?

How about putting on your bra? Are you able to put on your bra with the hooks in the back? This is something I hear from my patients on a regular basis. They have gotten so used to putting on their bra in the front that they don't even realize how limited their shoulder range of motion has become.

Treatment for this injury includes therapy, steroid injections and surgery. Most rotator cuff injuries are treated with physical therapy to strengthen the specific muscles that are weak and certain modalities that decrease inflammation and speed up healing.

Essentially, the treatment is to provide more balance to your shoulder joint that was undone with your bad posture. This is something you can help prevent now by improving the overall strength and stability of your rotator cuff.

LACK OF CONFIDENCE

Which came first; the bad posture or the lack of confidence? Visualize for a second how someone who is confident looks. How do they stand? How do they walk? Are they slouching? Slumping?

Now picture someone who is shy and less confident. *See what I mean?*

The vicious cycle of lack of confidence combined with bad posture goes on and on. People respond to you as if you have less confidence, or they have less confidence in you. *"You only get one chance to make a first impression"* so they say. What is your posture saying about you?

There is no time like the present to improve your posture and regain your confidence. It doesn't take many compliments on your posture to make a major change in how you feel about yourself.

LACK OF ENERGY

"Let me get this straight," you ask, *"I will have less energy if I have bad posture?"* Again the answer is a resounding **YES!** This may difficult to truly test out if you already have bad posture, but let's try something for a second.

Roll your shoulders forward and hunch. Stick your head forward. Take a deep breath.

Now, roll your shoulders back and stick out your chest. Do your best to put your head over your shoulders. Take a deep breath. Big difference, right? If you have bad posture, your entire day goes like this.

You see, in order for your body to generate energy for you, it must have oxygen. If you are unable to get the maximum amount of energy that your body needs to create the energy you need to get through your day, your energy levels will invariably drop.

I have a patient that is training at a very high level for running marathons. She is already someone in much better shape than most people dream about. Still, she had some posture issues that I couldn't help but to try and work on with her.

After a few days with some simple exercises, she noticed a change in her ability to breathe. *"I just take in fuller breaths,"* she said. **This posture stuff is amazing!**

LOOK HEAVIER AND OLDER

The more I thought about this, the more I realized these two descriptions were going to be based on the same thing. Are you actually older or heavier just because you have bad posture?

No, you just look that way. This has been determined by asking people to guess someone's age and weight just by looking at them. Almost across the board, when people had to guess the age of the person with bad posture, they guessed too high. In people with good posture, they were closer or lower than their actual age.

The same thing happened with regard to guessing a person's weight. In guessing the weight of the person with bad posture, the guesses tended to be higher than the person's actual weight. In good posture, the guesses were closer or lower.

Here's another experiment. Stand tall and take a deep breath in and out. Most likely you are tightening your abdominal muscles to accomplish this task. Compare that to what happens when you slouch.

Notice what happens when you roll your shoulders forward and curve your upper back. You end up relaxing your belling and it sticks out. You really can't help but look heavier with bad posture.

You can try to slouch and suck in your gut, but that is one intense exercise! You know you can't possibly sustain it.

Let's talk about some nutritional aspects of helping you with your posture.

"Is there anything I can eat to help me improve my posture?"

NUTRITION TO HELP YOUR POSTURE

Let's clarify something before we get started with this. You don't have bad posture because you may be overweight. I have patients that are skinny as a rail and are still convinced that they have bad posture because they *"need to lose a few pounds."*

If you happen to be overweight, I still don't say that your weight is causing your posture problem. Your weight issue is exaggerating your posture problem, but it did not cause it all by itself.

Still, the nutritional things we are going to be talking about here have nothing to do with losing weight, even though you will lose weight if you eat healthy foods. We are talking about the essential nutrients and supplements you need to support your muscles and get you on your way to the best posture you can achieve.

What would be the point of exercising your muscles and further straining yourself because poor nutrition has left your muscles totally depleted and unable to get stronger? Are you giving your muscles everything they need?

Even if you eat decently and are not in horrible shape, remembering some of these guidelines will be very helpful in speeding up your results. I know you want that.

PROTEIN

Protein is a critical component of every cell in your body. You need protein! Your body uses protein to build and repair every tissue in your body. Protein is also a primary component in your body's production of enzymes, hormones, and other vital chemicals. In addition, protein is the foundation of bones, muscles, cartilage, skin, and blood.

Different than fat, your body does not store protein. Extra protein does not build muscle (*only exercise can build muscle*), but getting a healthy amount of protein each day will go a long way in your body's ability to keep up the muscles you're going to be building by doing these exercises.

CALCIUM

Of course Calcium and Magnesium are taken to build up strong bones. If you're going to be placing extra stress and strain on your bones (*or have already for a long, long time*), they are going to need all the help they can get.

Magnesium enhances the absorption of Calcium, which can be very important. Why would you keep taking a vitamin that your body wouldn't absorb? How would you know? Giving your body the best chance to utilize the good stuff you're putting in it will give you the best results.

Over time, if your calcium intake is consistently less than your body's need, your body will leech the calcium from your bones. This ongoing process (*which has no symptom, by the way*) will lead to bone loss, eventually causing them to become weak and fracture easily.

Not having enough calcium just gets worse from there. Once your body has taken all the calcium it can from your bones (*the calcium is desperately needed for heart and blood functions, so your body's going to do what is has to do*), your joints become effected, then plaque starts to build up in the arteries, eventually this can potentially cause damage to your kidneys.

The following things inhibit the body's ability to absorb calcium and/or deplete your calcium supply:

- Caffeine
- Sugar
- Alcohol
- Smoking
- Aspirin
- Sedatives
- Barbituates
- Phosphoric acid (*found in soda, other carbonated drinks*)

Unfortunately, most of what we eat today is processed and has lost a lot of its nutritional value. While I would never suggest that we just eat bad and then supplement our way to good health, this is certainly something you should consider supplementing to your diet if you hope to get the amount of calcium your body needs.

GLUCOSAMINE

Glucosamine is a major component of joint cartilage, and is produced by your body. The glucosamine supplements available are made from shellfish and have been touted as a treatment for osteoarthritis (*inflammation of the joints*).

Glucosamine is believed to help slow the deterioration of cartilage, and increase the cartilage's ability to absorb water and increase elasticity. Glucosamine supplements are not cheap, and may take months to be truly effective. However, part of their effectiveness is in decreasing inflammation of the joints, which is why it's become such a sought after supplement for arthritis sufferers.

From a postural standpoint, if you've dealt with pain due to osteoarthritis and are now trying to improve your posture, this is likely a supplement that is right up your alley. Increasing the likelihood that you will achieve your goals of better posture and less back pain is why this supplement should be considered as part of your nutritional attack on your bad posture.

CHRONDROITIN

Chrondroitin is also a component of your cartilage and tendons. Chrondroitin supplements are derived from the cartilage of cows or sharks. The benefits of chondroitin include the reduction of inflammation and pain associated with osteoarthritis. Because of these benefits, most supplements include both glucosamine and chondroitin. The chondroitin supplement may also take months to work, similar to the glucosamine.

In addition to helping you with your overall joint health, chondroitin has been credited with the following:

- Increase ability to recover from injuries
- Reduced pain levels
- Reduced tenderness and swelling in the joints
- Increased flexibility and range of motion

- Improved connective tissue production and healing
- Increased bone healing and repair
- Improve your skin, including wrinkles and fine lines

OMEGA-3 FATTY ACIDS

Your typical Omega 3 supplements are produced from fish oil or flaxseed oil. Studies has shown that this supplement has the ability to reduce inflammation and can reduce the enzymes in your body that cause cartilage to break down.

SUMMARY

Again, the supplements we've included have a lot to do with healing up and reducing the pain in your joints. Part of this is to help heal the damage that you may have already caused with years of bad posture. The other part is to help you stay feeling good so that you can continue to due the exercises and get the fastest results possible.

I know that in improving your posture it is important not just that you get results, but that you get them quickly. The more "*good posture*" activities you perform, the better your results.

"Can't I just wear something that will fix my posture?"

POSTURE SUPPORTS

This may be most controversial part of this book. Most of the patients we encounter seem to think that they can just strap their shoulders back and their posture problem will be solved. This is a common misunderstanding and one that is very dangerous. The only thing saving most people is that they are so inconsistent wearing their posture supports that they never have a chance to suffer the complications.

Here's an example; in an attempt to lower the prevalence of back injuries suffered from heavy lifting, a local home improvement store issued back braces for all of their employees. The employees immediately begin wearing the back braces... the entire time they were on the job.

There was nothing inherently wrong with the back brace. It was a good back brace, it fit well and it supported the muscles of the low back and it supports the spine well. So what's the problem? What is the potential danger of wearing the back brace all the time?

You've heard the phrase *"use it or lose it."* This is absolutely true with regard to your muscles. If you are not using your muscles (*because they are in a brace all day*), they get weaker. It's not the kind of weakness that you're going to notice right away. Sure your muscles are getting weaker and weaker, but you keep putting on the brace and heading to work.

Over time, it was determined that the number of back injuries increased, not decreased with the use of these back braces. How is this possible? At the start of the back brace use, the muscles were stronger and then being additionally supported by the brace.

After awhile, the braces were supporting weaker and weaker backs, until eventually, the braces were the only things really holding everything together. The back injuries occurred not necessarily while lifting something, but in activities that shouldn't necessarily cause a back injury, like picking up a piece of paper off the floor. (*When not wearing the brace.*)

You'll still see them in use at this home improvement store, with one additional twist. They are loose around the waist of the employee until it's time to lift something. Then the brace is tightened, the object is lifted and then the brace is returned to its loose position.

Understanding this example, what do you think will happen to you if you have something strapped around your shoulders day in and day out? Will your shoulders and supporting muscles get stronger? Not in a million years.

We certainly understand why someone would seek out a posture brace. The pictures make it seem like its going to work fine. Put one on and your posture will look significantly better... for a short time.

On the other hand, posture supports like a good chair or good shoes are worth considering. The supports should not be drastic in the changes they are attempting to make. They should be there to help remind you and even to prevent you from assuming a bad postural position, but not to correct.

A low back support in your car while driving (*especially if you drive for considerable distances and your seat does not come with a built-in lumbar support feature*) should definitely be considered.

Good pillows and proper support while you sleep is also key and well covered in other areas of this book.

The main conclusion here is that posture supports are designed to do just that, support. They are not the answer to your posture correction needs. If they are too dramatic in what they are trying to change, they could also end up causing more harm then good.

You're going to keep reading this book looking for alternatives to exercise as the way to changing your posture, but you're not going to find it. How else are you going to get your muscles to support your body?

"So, if I do the exercises they can fix all of my posture problems?"

POSTURE PROBLEMS THAT CAN'T BE FIXED
(*At Least Not On Your Own...*)

HERNIATED DISC

While we covered the *"what is a herniated disc?"* in the section on the effects of bad posture, we'll briefly cover why you can't fix this condition on your own. If you've skipped ahead to this section, you'll want to go back review more information on a herniated disc in the prior sections.

The term *"herniated disc"* is super-scary to most of the patients that come into our office. They are usually worried if they have one, and then run off as quickly as possible to a surgeon if they find out they do have, in fact, a herniated disc.

There are alternatives to caring for herniated disc that don't involve surgery, although surgery is sometimes required.

MEDICATION

Some patients are prescribed medications to control pain or to decrease inflammation. Sometimes muscle relaxants are prescribed. Keep in mind that covering up the symptoms with medication can lead to further problems. How do you know if you're better? How do you know if what you're doing right now is helping or hurting you?

The "best case" scenario for taking medications is that the decrease in inflammation gives your disc a chance to heal. Also, managing the pain can give you a chance to actually do something about some of the structural problems that may be contributing to the condition.

CHIROPRACTIC AND PHYSICAL THERAPY

Depending on the severity of the herniated disc, chiropractic and physical therapy should be considered prior to even seriously considering surgery. Most primary care physicians will recommend a regimen of therapy prior to considering surgery.

In most cases, the therapy that is recommended by your medical doctor will be physical therapy, not chiropractic. If the physical therapy gets some results, but you still find that you are having problems, chiropractic care should still be considered.

Injections are another stepping stone in the herniated disc process of treatment and resolution. Usually the injections are performed in a series of three, with the pain medication being injected directly into the area of pain.

In any case, <u>all</u> possible treatments should be considered before surgery is performed.

SURGERY

The goal of surgery is to remove any portion of the disc that may be pressing on or irritating spinal nerves. It is the pressure on spinal nerves that contributes significantly to pain, weakness, or the numbness and tingling.

The most common procedure involves removing all or part of the disc. Less often, a portion of the vertebra is removed to make more room for the disc. A small percentage of patients will have their disc herniated again, despite the surgery.

We believe most surgery can be avoided if the symptoms are listened to early enough. Achieving good posture and not letting persistent back pain go unchecked can alleviate this problem. Do not ignore your back pain, and take action if you suspect you may be heading down the path of a herniated disc.

SCOLIOSIS

First of all, spinal misalignments and scoliosis are not the same thing. Many patients come to my office with a concern that they have scoliosis. When we take an x-ray and it reveals that their curves are not as they should be, the first assumption is that they have scoliosis.

Scoliosis is a largely hereditary condition. It's not a guarantee that if someone in your family has scoliosis that you'll get it too, but it certainly increases the chances (*by about 20%*).

The vast majority of scoliosis is called "*idiopathic*," which is a fancy way of saying "*unknown cause*." This type usually develops prior to puberty and is more prevalent in girls than boys. Scoliosis can develop in adults, but is usually a non-diagnosed and/or non-treated version of a childhood condition.

Adult scoliosis can also develop as a result of spinal deformities and complications resulting from osteporosis.

Parents should watch for the following signs of scoliosis (*If you think you have any of these, you may also question of you just have bad posture or bad posture with scoliosis.*):

- Uneven shoulders
- Uneven base of the head (*sometimes your earrings make this more noticeable.*)
- Prominent shoulder blade or shoulder blades
- Uneven waist
- Elevated hips
- Leaning to one side

If a scoliotic curve is severe when it is first seen, or if treatment with a brace does not control the curve, surgery may be necessary. There are scoliosis-focused chiropractors out there that have seen good success in treating this condition. As always, surgery should be considered only as a last option.

SPINAL FRACTURE

While you can certainly get a spinal fracture due to a significant trauma, here we're evaluating a spinal fracture due to a complication from osteoporosis. Essentially, the bone becomes weak and then begins to collapse under your own body weight.

Many times the fracture is never diagnosed and found years later on an x-ray. The main symptom of a spinal fracture is back pain. The back pain is similar to any other strain or common back injury.

So the patient takes their medications and hopes it goes away... and it does. Fractures heal like anything else and even a spinal fracture will heal. However, now that the patient has weak bones and one less vertebra to support the weight, more spinal fractures often result.

Spinal fractures due to osteoporosis often occur while doing something that causes relatively minor trauma to the spine, such as an insignificant fall, or twisting while lifting. Even such activities as sneezing, coughing, or turning over in bed can lead to compression fractures in advanced osteoporosis.

Ultimately, it's these fractures that severely alter the shape of the spine, leading to thoracic hyperkyphosis also known as a dowager's hump. Avoiding osteoporosis is obviously a key component to decreasing your chance of spinal fracture.

Improving your posture and decreasing the strain on weak vertebrae is extremely important in avoiding this problem.

MISSHAPEN VERTEBRA

While not a large percentage, there are those people that were born with a vertebra or vertebrae that are not shaped normally. While this may not be life-threatening, painful, or even noticeable, it may cause poor posture.

Before you blame your bad posture on the shape of your vertebrae, remember that just because your vertebra is shaped differently, it doesn't mean that this is the cause of your posture problems.

However, if you are working at improving your posture and it just doesn't seem to make any difference, it may be that you're working with a structural problem that cannot be exercised back into place.

Let's not totally disregard the right exercises for you just because you think that maybe, possibly, you have a misshapen vertebra. You'll need to visit your family doctor or chiropractor to get an x-ray to be sure.

SPONDYLOLISTHESIS

Spondylolisthesis is a condition of the spine in which one vertebra *"slips"* over the vertebra below it. There are various causes, including stress fracture to a part of the vertebra and age-related degenerative changes.

A stress fracture in a vertebra may cause it to disconnect from its facet joints. The vertebra slips forward, leading to misalignment and narrowing of the spinal canal. A x-ray will indicate the level involved and the severity.

Spondylolisthesis is usually treated well with conservative treatment, including chiropractic care. Surgery is rarely needed. If you are experiencing back pain (*particularly sharp pain*) following exercise, this is yet another thing to consider.

Consult with your healthcare professional or other "*improve your posture*" practitioner and get the right program for you.

"If I need help improving my posture, who are the best people to ask in my area?"

"IMPROVE YOUR POSTURE" PRACTITIONERS

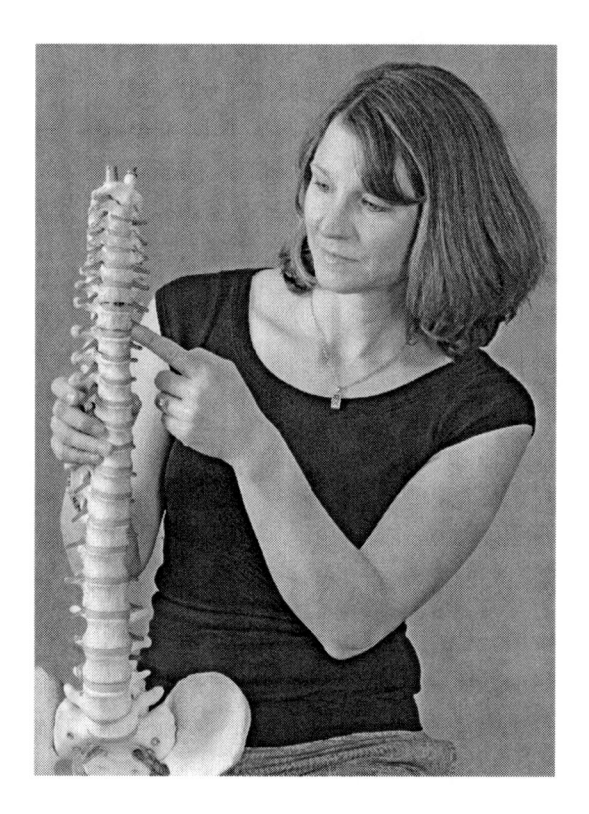

Given that many posture conditions are going to need a little extra help, I've put together the most likely prospects in helping you get to your posture goals. I stress again that if you do the exercises and watch your posture, you should do fine.

However, if you are not getting the results you want and you are concerned that you may have a condition that can't be fixed by exercise, these *"improve your posture"* practitioners have specialized areas that can be of assistance.

CHIROPRACTIC

Chiropractic can be very beneficial when your spine has become involved in your poor posture – especially if you've had it for a long time. If you hold an improper position too long, your spinal joints can become fixated or stuck in the wrong position.

In particular, if you find that you are simply unable to *"stand up straight,"* that it is no longer even up to your memory to get this done, that you are stuck or locked in the forward hunching position,… it is time to visit a chiropractor.

Your bones are likely stuck and out of alignment. This is not something you should try to take care of yourself.

A chiropractic adjustment finds the area of your spine (*it's usually not the entire spine*) that is out of alignment and helps restore the normal position and function. That "pop" you might hear (*there are non-"popping" ways to move your spine*), is your vertebra becoming unstuck. Yeah!

You can probably make your bones *"pop,"* but please don't do it around me. Each vertebra can move out of place up to 16 different ways. Unless you're a chiropractor, you likely have no idea which way it has moved. As such, you have no idea the direction it needs to move in order to go back to its proper location. So don't do it!

When you have your friend bear-hug you at the family barbeque and lift you up and down, resulting in a chorus of *"pops,"* you have not done a good thing. I know, I know, it feels better. The reason for that is the *"pop"* has released your body's own natural pain killers, namely endorphins and enkephalins. These substances are released even when the vertebra is moved the wrong way, and even if the vertebra you moved didn't need to move in the first place.

Here's the way some people get their back *"cracked."* (*It gives me the chills.*) They… let… other people… walk on their backs. Oops! Is that you? Please stop doing that too. Again, your spine is designed to move and function a specific way. Moving it the wrong way is not what we're going for.

When a Chiropractor performs a chiropractic adjustment, they are not only moving the vertebra the right direction, they are moving just the one that needs to move! We use small bones in our hands or special instruments to accomplish this. Someone's foot is no where near as specific. How could it be? (*Not that the person doing the stomping has any idea which direction they were hoping to move the vertebra.*)

Okay, so adjusting your own spine is bad. Letting a trained Doctor of Chiropractic do it is good. Once you've undergone a chiropractic treatment plan, you still need to do the exercises to keep your spine in good shape and your posture up to par.

Chiropractors also can help with some of the conditions I've indicated that you can't fix on your own. Your posture is the window to your spine, who better to take a look at your spine than a chiropractor?

PHYSICAL THERAPY

If you don't think you can follow through with the exercises on your own, physical therapy may be a route to consider. My goal is to see you have the best posture you can have for as long as possible. Sometimes you just need a jumpstart.

Unless you get a referral from you physician and your insurance covers it, physical therapy will not be cheap.

However, it is part of the practice of physical therapy to evaluate posture and determine an exercise program to help correct what is needed. The physical therapist can use exercise, stretching, massage, and other muscle and soft tissue techniques to accomplish this goal.

Make sure your find a physical therapist that will provide "*active*" care. Some may have you on "*passive*" care like ultrasound and electric muscle stimulation. While passive care is great for new injuries, they will not help your posture. You're going to have to do active things (*like exercise*) to make a change.

The physical therapist is going to make you exercise. Hmm... where have you heard that before?

MASSAGE

Massage can certainly be helpful in relaxing your muscles, but are not going to strengthen your muscles. In particular, the "relaxing" massage will likely do nothing to alleviate your posture issue.

With poor posture, certain muscles get overworked. These muscles fatigue, spasm, and then harden as a result. Massage can relax these muscles, increase the blood flow to the area and decrease the rate of degeneration.

Deep tissue massage is going to be the more helpful massage technique to have performed. While this type of massage can be painful, the benefits will last much longer than the non-deep tissue massage. "No pain, no gain" is appropriate here.

Speaking of painful massage, a technique called Rolfing is also adept at making postural changes in the spine. Rolfers are not the easiest to find, but there is usually at least one practitioner in any major city.

Receiving a Rolfing massage is a deep tissue massage on another level. While we already discussed that the deep tissue massage can be painful, this session will be as well. Since the practitioner is going deeper, the benefits will last even longer than the deep tissue massage.

A massage related practitioner is known as a "*rolfer*." Named for the originator, Dr. Ida Rolf, "*rolfers*" seek to align the entire body by manipulating the muscles and connective tissue of the spine. My personal experience with rolfing has been almost totally positive.

While the working of the fascia and connective tissue can be painful, the rolfer shows your proper ways to breathe to eliminate the pain. The results are good, and last a long time. I did have one situation in which a patient sought out rolfing while dealing with a severely inflamed low back condition and just wasn't quite ready to undergo that type of treatment.

Still, if your body needs a major overhaul to get your posture going in the right direction, this is something that should be considered.

And, yes, after that you still need to do the exercises!

YOGA

There is more to yoga than just getting more flexible, for sure. Yoga has its own philosophy including the view that a person's posture reflects their mental, emotional, and spiritual state.

Yoga requires strength and flexibility, something that if you don't have, you will soon obtain if you perform the exercises regularly. Yoga exercises are meant to be performed as gentle stretching with a feeling of relaxation. According to yoga practitioners, if you are sore afterward, you are not quite doing it right.

Even though this is a very simple explanation of what yoga is, the primary benefit of practicing yoga for the average person is improved flexibility. Certainly, getting together with a group of people to be healthy and improve posture will be beneficial your pursuit of better health.

PILATES

Developed by Joseph Pilates, this exercise was designed to improve strength and flexibility without becoming "*bulky.*" Pilates has enjoyed increased popularity with the more recent focus on improving one's "core." Pilates develops abdominal strength, improving your spinal support.

There are Pilates programs popping up everywhere, including home-study courses. Generally, there are two types; floor pilates and classes utilizing reformers. Both are very beneficial.

Pilates is another form of exercise. I hope you are starting to see that you are going to have to exercise to make effective and lasting change to your posture.

"Which muscles are used in maintaining good posture?"

POSTURE ANATOMY

No description of your postural anatomy would be complete without the spine. We deal with this very important structure all day long! In a nutshell, you have 7 cervical vertebrae (neck), which should have a lordotic curve.

You have 12 thoracic vertebrae (*mid back*) that should have a kyphotic curve. You also have 5 lumbar vertebrae (*low back*) which should also have a lordotic curve similar to the curve in your neck.

The pelvis makes up the last portion of your spinal column, made up of two bigger pieces of bone met in the middle by your sacrum. Where the joints meet up on each side is referred to as your sacroiliac joints.

All of the exercises that make up this book are done in an effort to stretch or strengthen various aspects of the spine's surrounding musculature. Most importantly, the exercises are there to help maintain and support the natural curves of the spine.

Do this, and you have a great foundation for good health.

In the following sections, we will go over the key muscles that affect your posture. We will explain how to stretch or strengthen the muscles indicated and give a demonstration of that exercise.

This is meant to give you a general overview of the postural muscles and to be able to work on just the muscle you may need to improve. In later sections, we demonstrate exercise routines that will make changes to specific postural syndromes. You may still want to add in one or two more specific muscles into the outlined routines.

RHOMBOIDS

These muscles attach the shoulder blades to the spine. With bad posture, these muscles tend to get overstretched and weakened. They are the muscles that must be targeted in order to pull those shoulders back. When they are too long, they shoulder blades tend roll forward and that will roll the shoulders in.

This is definitely a muscle to strengthen, not stretch. You have two rhomboid muscles, one on each side of your spine connecting to your shoulder blade.

Starting Position: Arms out to your side, full extending your arms with your elbows bent.

Exercise: Focus on bringing your shoulder blades together and slightly down. This movement will naturally cause your arms to go back 2 to 3 inches. Hold for a count of "1" and perform 3 sets of 15.

Starting Position: Side View

Exercise: Side View

LATISSMUS DORSI

The latissmus dorsi is the largest muscle in the body, and acts to bring the humerus (*upper arm*) down from a raised position. It is also responsible for internally rotating your upper arm.

Starting Position: Arms out to your side, full extending your arms with your elbows bent. Arms should be slightly above your shoulders.

Exercise: Focus on bringing your shoulder blades down and into the spine. Bring your elbows down, squeezing hard and moving them slightly behind your body. Hold for a count of "1" and return to the starting position. 3 sets of 15.

94   *Posture Confidence: Everything You Need To Change Your Posture For Good*

Starting Position: Rear View

Exercise: Rear View

PARASPINALS

The muscles directly on either side of your spine are called the paraspinals. These muscles support and move the spine. There are many small muscles joining each vertebra to the next as well as larger muscles that are more relevant in posture.

Starting Position: Standing, arms above your head.

Exercise: Focus on contracting the muscles along your spine. Your arms should go back 4 – 6". Raise your chin up approximately 30 degrees. Bring your shoulder blades down and back. Hold for a count of "1" and return to the starting position. Perform 3 sets of 15 repetitions.

Starting Position: Side View

Exercise: Side View

PSOAS

The psoas muscle is responsible for stabilizing the base of the spine. The psoas allows the spine to flex (bend forward) and helps in rotating the hips.

Starting Position: Arms on hips. One foot forward, pelvis straight with no rotation. Your other foot is behind you.

Exercise: Stretch this muscle by lunging slightly forward and focusing on the knee going down toward the floor. Your goal is to extend the hip and not to stretch your calf. Hold for a count of "20."

SCM & SCALENES

You have two SCM muscles, one on each side of your neck. Each muscle runs from the sternum (*chest bone*) and your clavicle (*collar bone*) and to the mastoid (*part of the skull behind your ear*).

The scalenes are found from the first and second ribs up through the side of the neck. There are three scalenes, the anterior, medius, and posterior.

Exercise: Tilt your head to the side and slightly up. Place your hands on the muscle at your chest and collar bone. This allows you to traction that muscle more specifically. To stretch additional muscle fibers, tilt your chin slightly down and up while tilting your head to the side. Remember to alternate sides.

Stretch both at the same time by pulling down on the skin under each collar bone, then tilting your head gently back.

You will feel areas of more tension to let you know what needs more attention. Stop if you feel dizzy. You may want to sit for extra stability if you feel your neck is vulnerable. Hold for a count of "5."

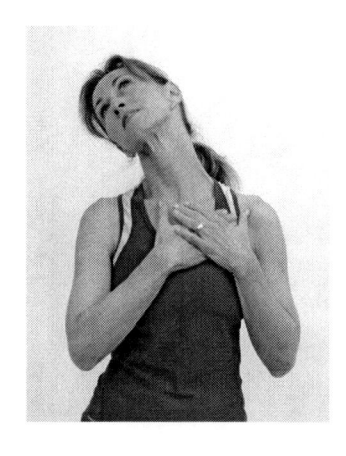

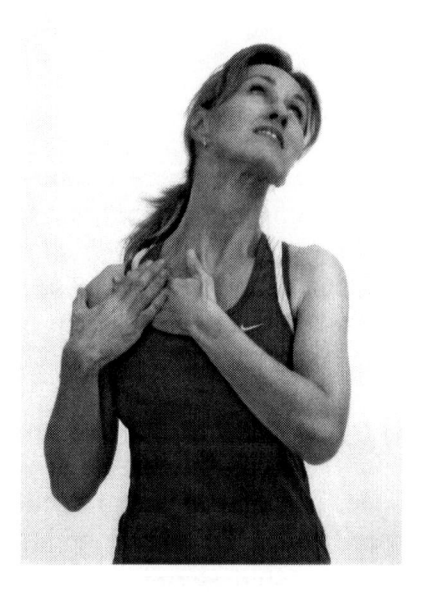

102 *Posture Confidence: Everything You Need To Change Your Posture For Good*

(2)

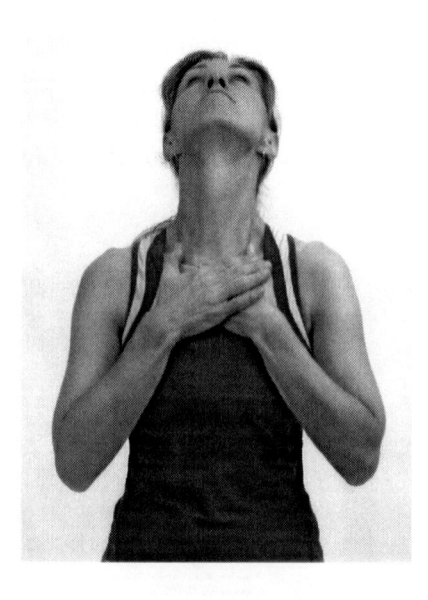

(3)

TRAPEZIUS

There are three areas of the trapezius muscle; upper fibers, middle fibers, and lower fibers. Each division helps out in performing actions that include moving the shoulder blade up, down and towards your spine, bringing the head and neck backward and assisting in movements needed for breathing.

Starting Position: Draw up your shoulders as close to your ears as possible, contracting your trapezius muscles. Hold for a count of "5."

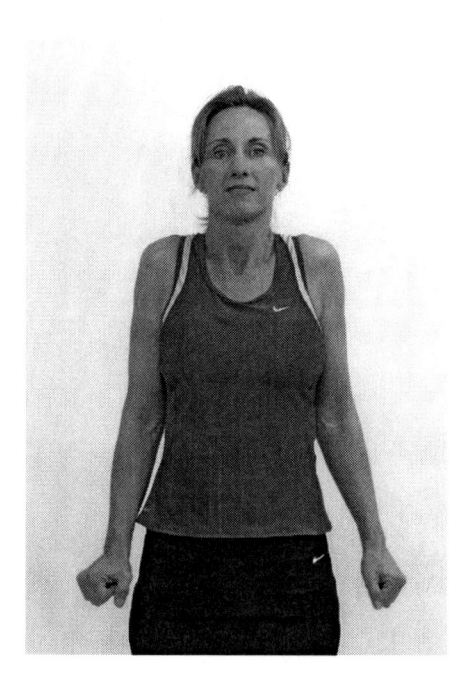

Exercise: Pull shoulders down as far as you can to help stretch and elongate this muscle. Hold for a count of "5."

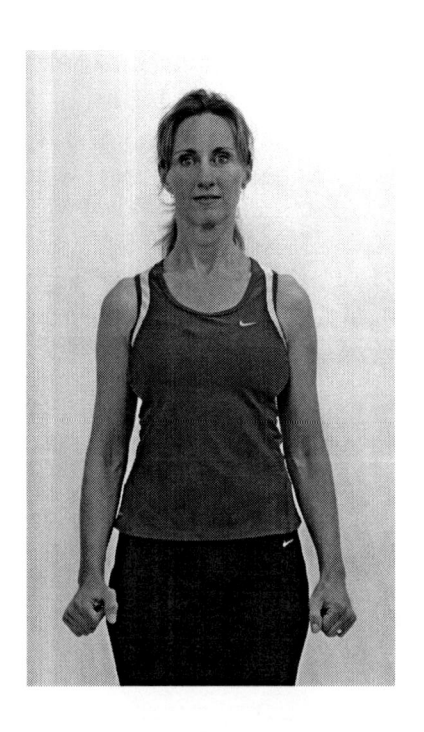

PECTORALIS

The pectoralis major muscle makes up the greatest portion of your chest muscles. It is a thick, fan-shaped muscle that is primarily responsible for pushing. This muscle is also focused on whenever someone decides to hit the gym, which can lead to bad posture.

Bad posture due to overdeveloping your pectoralis muscle (*combined with underdeveloping the back muscles*) is a huge chunk of why people end up with bad posture, even if they're working out.

Starting Position: Find a doorway. The drawback here is that the doorway is a fixed size. The size may or may not be ideal for you. Remember to do both sides.

Exercise:

1. *Inferior Pecs*: Raise hand to where shoulder is almost fully extended. Again elbow is still supported by the wall. Lean forward. Stretch out the lower part of the pectoralis. (*You are also stretching your latissmus.*) Hold for a count of "20."

2. *Middle Pecs*: Hand and elbow should contact the door frame. Lean forward and stretch out the pectoralis muscles for a count of "20."

3. Superior Pecs: Lower arm to where hand is level with your shoulder. Elbow is almost bent completely. Lean forward. Focus on stretching the top part of your pectoralis. Hold for a count of "20."

(1)

(2)

(3)

SUPRASPINATUS

Starting Position: Stand with good posture holding a light weight in each hand (optional). Starting with your right hand, hold the weight as if you're about to pull out your sword.

Keep your arm slightly bent while "pulling out your sword." You should feel the muscles at the back of your shoulder being used.

Exercise: Focus on contracting this small muscle at the back of your shoulder, on top of your shoulder blade. Raise arms up and back, keeping the elbows slightly bent. 3 sets of 15, use light weight.

Starting Position: Side View

Exercise: Side View

TERES MINOR

Starting Position: Stand straight with your back and abdominals tight. Shoulder blades are pulled back and down. Arms are down at your side with your elbows bent at 90 degrees.

Exercise: Rotate your arms away from your midline, keeping your elbows at your side. Contract the muscles that draw your arm back and squeeze. 3 sets of 15.

Starting Position: Side View

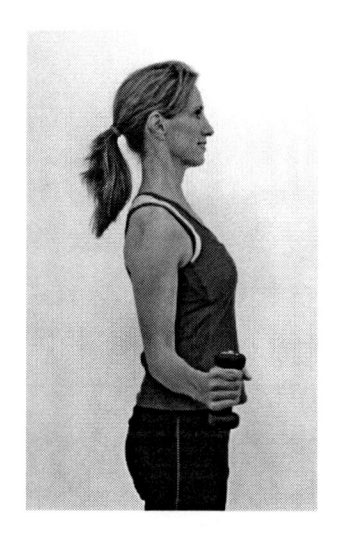

Exercise: Side View

ABDOMINALS

I think most everyone can point to where their abdominals are (*or least where they are supposed to be*). You may not realize that your abdominal muscles are actually a group of 6 muscles that extend from your ribs to various places on your pelvis. They provide support and movement for the trunk of your body as well as assist in helping you breathe.

Upper Abdominals

Starting Position: Lay face up with your knees bent and your feet on the floor. Arms out to your side, elbows bent and your hand by your ears. Do not put your hands behind your neck. All the work needs to be done with your abs and the neck should be one solid unit. Upper shoulders and neck are slightly off the floor.

Exercise: Contract your abs, raising your upper body slightly up. You can really strengthen this muscle without raising and flexing your entire upper body. 40 reps.

ALTERNATIVE

Starting Position: Cross your arms over your upper body. All else remains the same. This should help you to isolate the abdominals and limit the flexion of your neck and head. It is not the head that leads this exercise.

Exercise: Contract your abs, raising your upper body slightly up. 40 reps.

Upper and Lower Abdominals

Integrating the upper and lower abs strengthens the continuity of this muscle group.

Starting Position: Laying face up, bring up one arm up with your hand near your ear. Your other arm remains at your side. Raise the opposite knee with your leg slightly stretched away from your body.

Exercise: Contract your abdominals, bringing your elbow to the opposite knee. Your upper body is raised and twisted slightly toward the midline of your body. Stop at the point where you stopped while doing your upper abs. 20 reps per side.

Lower Abdominals

Starting Position: Lay face up with your legs flexed at the hips and your feet up in the air. Arms are at your side.

Exercise: Contract the lower abs while raising your legs higher in the air. Bottom is listed off the ground by 2 to 3". Keep your spine tight and straight. 40 reps.

ALTERNATIVE

Starting Position: Lay face up with your legs raised off the ground 2". Arms are at your side and may be used as support by putting your hands under your bottom.

Exercise: Contract your lower abs while raising your feet up into the air about 18". Keep your spine tight and straight. 40 reps.

Lateral Abdominals

Starting Position: Lay on your side with your top arm bent and your hand by your ear. Your opposite arm should be on your lateral abdominals to feel the muscle contract. Your lower body is slightly bent at the hips, knees, and feet. Your upper body is slightly rotated back.

Exercise: Contract your lateral abs and raise your upper body about 4". Hold for a count of "1." 40 reps per side.

DIAGNOSE YOUR POSTURE PROBLEM

How are you going to fix your bad posture? Time to take a hard look at your posture. It's not enough to determine that you have bad posture, but what exactly is bad about it? In the exercise portion of this book, we have broken down the most common bad posture conditions along with a *"general posture improvement"* program. In addition, you'll find a specific exercise or two to improve a specific muscle, if needed.

Time for a postural analysis, what is it you think needs your attention? This is a difficult process to get totally straight on your own. We suggest finding someone to help you take a look.

By yourself, you can get a head start by looking at yourself in the mirror. Do your shoulders seem to roll forward, or are they back. Can you even move them back if you want to, or are they stuck?

Check out the level of your ears, compare side to side. Check your shoulder heights, are they also even side to side? Lastly, dig into your sides, the "love handle" areas. Feel for the tops of your pelvis. Once you've found them on each side, mark the top with your hands. Now you have a rough idea about the height of your pelvis from side to side.

All three of these things (*ears, shoulders, pelvis*) are good posture landmarks to evaluate how you're doing from the front. How are you going to check yourself from the side on your own? Other than rigging up some sort of camera/mirror combo, it's just easiest to find a helper.

Stand as naturally as possible, (*you can try it again attempting to do your best possible posture*), and take a look. Your most natural posture is obviously more likely to represent how you look most of the time during your normal activities.

Your ear lobe should line up with your shoulder, which should line up with your hip down to your ankle. Does your posture do that?

FORWARD HEAD POSTURE

This is sometimes referred to as "military neck" or "vulture neck." Your head juts forward, and it makes it look like your neck is longer than it actually is.

Your ear lobe is in front of your shoulders. It's possible that your ear lobe will still line up with your shoulders if they are also rolled forward, but your head will appear more forward than your shoulders.

Is this you? Then you will benefit from working on the exercises to head and neck posture. Once the neck muscles become strained, leaning your head over for even short periods of times can lead to neck pain.

Proper posture allows strained neck and back muscles to heal more quickly.

ROUNDED SHOULDERS

Are your shoulders in front of your head, hip, and ankle? Are you having trouble rolling your shoulders back? Are you already beginning to show signs of hyperkyphosis aka *"the hump"*?

If your shoulders are rounded you need to stretch the chest muscles and strengthen your upper back muscles. Rounded shoulders are usually the result of slouching.

When slouching, the natural forward curve of the neck is exaggerated, which often results in neck pain as and upper back pain. Slouching is more common when sitting, and is often caused by fatigue, especially when sitting in front of a computer.

"THE HUMP" (Dowager Hump)

Particularly with osteoporosis, vertebrae become fragile and fracture. If the fracture occurs in the front half of the vertebra (*more common with typical bad postural positions and the increased stress with that posture*), the vertebra above will begin to tilt forward.

This continues to increase the likelihood of additional fractures, more tilting, and further advancement of the dowager's hump.

This condition is the most serious of all posture problems, as it can reach a point where the damage is no longer reversible. You can end up with a condition that you are simply working hard just to keep it from getting worse.

The dowager hump is bad posture + osteoporosis. Your best option is to begin going after this condition from all fronts; nutritionally, exercise, and with supports.

EXERCISES

The exercise portion of this book has been designed to give you a ready-made posture improving routine for your specific condition.

It is recommended that you perform the exercises for *"General Posture Improvement"* as a starting point. If you have more of the forward head posture, rounded shoulders, or are worried about the dowager hump, you can do the *"Improving Neck & Shoulder Posture"* in addition to the general exercises (*but not necessarily on the same day*).

If you were looking for more and more exercises to be made available to you, I assure you more exercises are not necessary to get the results you need.

If you were looking for exercises that are very complicated and difficult to perform, you do not understand that it is your simple, boring daily activities that got you this way in the first place. It is really more important to do the exercises outlined here to counteract your normal daily activities. They need not be complicated to work incredibly well.

Give the exercises a consistent effort. When done daily, you should begin to notice a difference in your ability to stand up straight and pain and discomfort will begin to fade in just days. Do these exercises every day for a month and you will be amazed at the difference in your posture.

Some people still think that just because they work out all the time, they don't need exercises as uncomplicated as these. We could go to the gym right now and find people in great shape and full of muscles… with horrible posture. What are they missing from their exercise regimen? Take a look at the exercises listed here for your answer.

As always, should you experience pain (*particularly sharp pain*)… **STOP!** Some soreness is okay and is to be expected when starting out with any exercise program. If you are very sore, you should back off the repetitions or the frequency of the exercises.

If you have further questions, please consult with your chiropractor, medical doctor, or other trusted healthcare professional.

EXERCISES FOR GENERAL POSTURE IMPROVEMENT

Each exercise is an intense focus on a small area. Make each repetition a focus on the exercise part, and relax as you return to the neutral (*starting*) position.

The goal of these exercises is to balance out the front, side, and back muscles. You may notice that you can do many more abdominal crunches, but the back or sides fatigue faster. Most people have so much more strength in their abdominals compared to their backs because of the activities we do everyday that keep us hunched over.

Take note of how many abdominal crunches you can do, and let that be your goal number for other areas. You may have to limit the number of abdominal exercises you do until the other areas get a chance to catch up. Otherwise you can just end up making your bad posture worse!

Soon you will see that your weaker areas are getting stronger. As you strengthen all areas, you should strive to develop all areas equally. This is the key to balance and the key to good posture.

GENERAL POSTURE IMPROVEMENT

EXERCISE 1: **Upper Abdominals**

Starting Position: Lay face up with your knees bent and your feet on the floor. Arms out to your side, elbows bent and your hand by your ears. Do not put your hands behind your neck. All the work needs to be done with your abs and the neck should be one solid unit. Upper shoulders and neck are slightly off the floor.

Exercise: Contract your abs, raising your upper body slightly up. You can really strengthen this muscle without raising and flexing your entire upper body. 40 reps.

ALTERNATIVE

Starting Position: Cross your arms over your upper body. All else remains the same. This should help you to isolate the abdominals and limit the flexion of your neck and head. It is not the head that leads this exercise.

Exercise: Contract your abs, raising your upper body slightly up. 40 reps.

GENERAL POSTURE IMPROVEMENT

EXERCISE 2:   Upper & Lower Abs

Starting Position: Laying face up, bring up one arm up with your hand near your ear. Your other arm remains at your side. Raise the opposite knee with your leg slightly stretched away from your body.

Exercise: Contract your abdominals, bringing your elbow to the opposite knee. Your upper body is raised and twisted slightly toward the midline of your body. Stop at the point where you stopped while doing your upper abs. 20 reps per side.

GENERAL POSTURE IMPROVEMENT

EXERCISE 3: Lower Abdominals

Starting Position: Lay face up with your legs flexed at the hips and your feet up in the air. Arms are at your side.

Exercise: Contract the lower abs while raising your legs higher in the air. Bottom is listed off the ground by 2 to 3". Keep your spine tight and straight. 40 reps.

ALTERNATIVE

Starting Position: Lay face up with your legs raised off the ground 2". Arms are at your side and may be used as support by putting your hands under your bottom.

Exercise: Contract your lower abs while raising your feet up into the air about 18". Keep your spine tight and straight. 40 reps.

GENERAL POSTURE IMPROVEMENT

EXERCISE 4: Lateral Abdominals

Starting Position: Lay on your side with your top arm bent and your hand by your ear. Your opposite arm should be on your lateral abdominals to feel the muscle contract. Your lower body is slightly bent at the hips, knees, and feet. Your upper body is slightly rotated back.

Exercise: Contract your lateral abs and raise your upper body about 4". Hold for a count of "1." 40 reps per side.

GENERAL POSTURE IMPROVEMENT

EXERCISE 5: Outer Thigh

Starting Position: Start out lying on your side. Your bottom leg is slightly bent for support, while your top leg is straight. The top leg is raised 2 to 3" above the bottom leg. Your bottom arm can support your head up.

If this hurts, or you are more comfortable with your head in a more neutral position, then do that. The top arm comes forward to support your balance. Adding a slight lean forward may also be helpful.

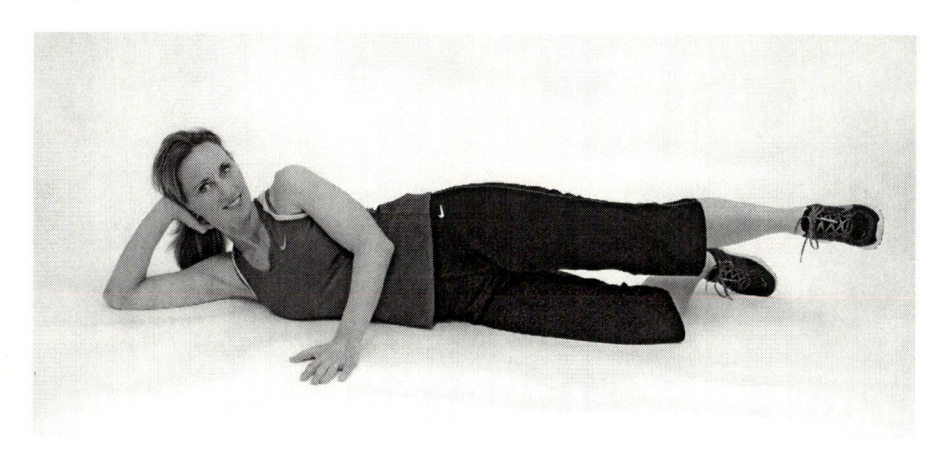

Exercise: Raise your leg 4 to 5", contracting the outer thigh. Keep the knee and foot facing forward. Hold for a count of "1" and return to starting position. 40 reps per side.

GENERAL POSTURE IMPROVEMENT

EXERCISE 6: Gluteals

Starting Position: Start on your side again. Bend your bottom leg for support and keep the top leg straight. If you experience any pain in your knees while performing this exercise, try turning on your stomach and then raise your leg with the knee bent. Have your top leg elevated above the bottom leg by 2 to 3". Remember to do both sides.

Exercise: Use your top hand to help resist the change in weight distribution and push your leg back. Contract your glute (butt) muscles and your hamstrings. Hold for a count of "1" and return to neutral position. 40 reps.

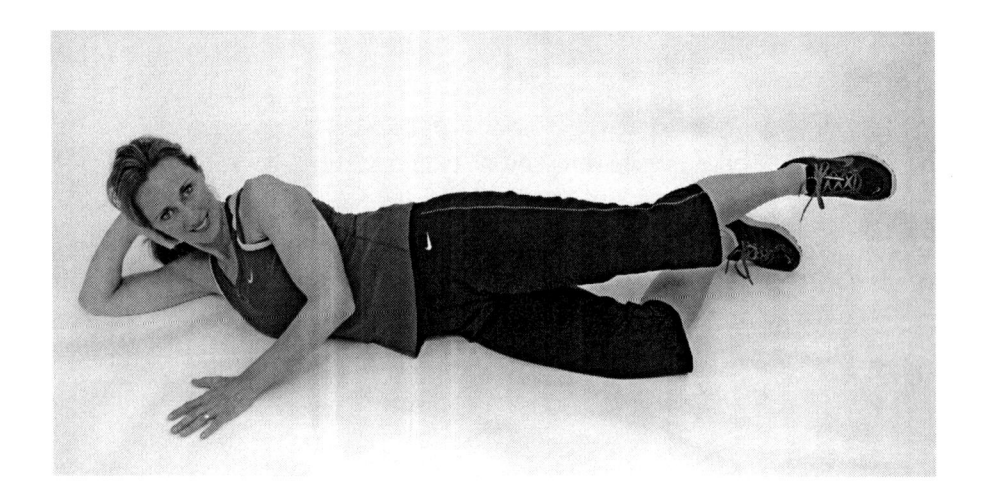

GENERAL POSTURE IMPROVEMENT

EXERCISE 7: Back

Starting Position: Lay down on your stomach. Arms should be extended straight over your head and your legs should be straight back.

Exercise: Raise your upper body and neck off the ground 4 to 5". For a more advanced option, raise your upper body and lower body at the same time. 2 sets of 40.

GENERAL POSTURE IMPROVEMENT

EXERCISE 8: Back

Starting Position: Lay down on your stomach. Arms should be extended straight over your head and your legs should be straight back. Elevate your left arm and your right leg off the ground.

Exercise: Raise your left arm up 4 to 6" more and the right leg 4 to 6" more. Hold for a count of "1" and return to starting position. Repeat 10 times, then switch to the right arm and left leg. 2 sets of 20 per side.

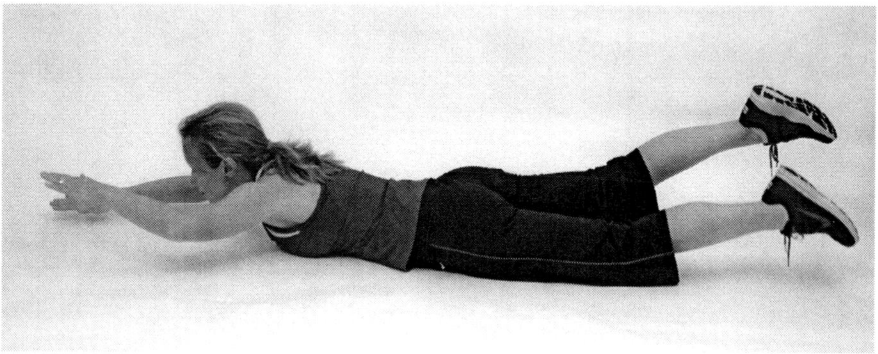

GENERAL POSTURE IMPROVEMENT

EXERCISE 9: Rhomboids

Starting Position: Lay down on your stomach with your arms out to your sides. Raise your upper body off the ground 2 to 3".

Exercise: Raise your upper body 4 to 6" and bring your elbows straight up (*toward the ceiling*). Contract the muscles to bring your shoulder blades as close to your spine as possible. Hold for a count of "1" and return to starting position. 2 set s of 40.

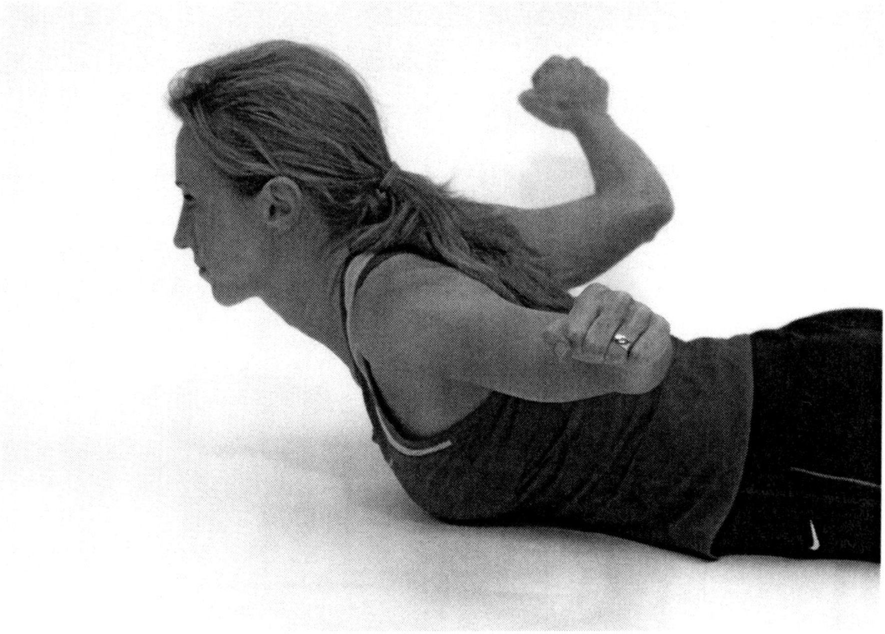

GENERAL POSTURE IMPROVEMENT

EXERCISE 10: Latissmus Dorsi

Starting Position: Lay down on your stomach with your arms out to your sides. Raise your upper body off the ground 2 to 3".

Exercise: Raise your upper body 4 to 6" and bring your elbows down toward your waist. Contract your lats to lower your arms and move your shoulder blades down and toward your spine. 2 sets of 40.

Natalie A. Cordova | Philip V. Cordova

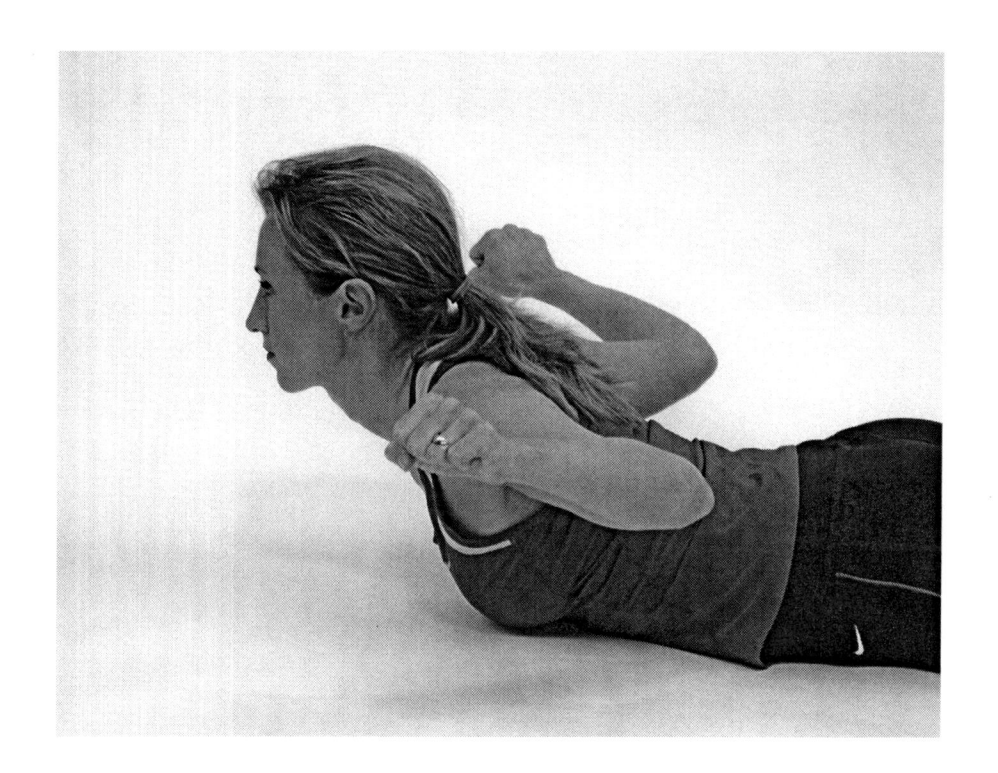

GENERAL POSTURE IMPROVEMENT

EXERCISE 11: Front and Back

Starting Position/Exercise: Face down, body weight is supported by elbows, lift yourself off the ground. Hold for a count of 60 seconds or until you can no longer hold it. Keep your abs tight and your body straight. Do not arch your low back.

GENERAL POSTURE IMPROVEMENT

EXERCISE 12: Back

Starting Position: Face down, arms down by your side. Palms are up. Raise your upper body slightly.

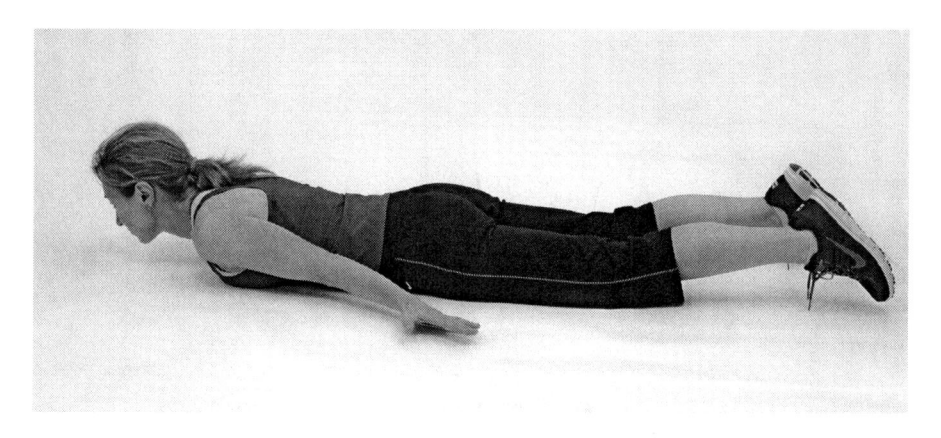

Exercise: Raise your body 4 to 6", rotating your hands externally until your palms are face down. Squeeze your shoulder blades together and contract your back muscles. Hold for a count of "1." Return to neutral position. 2 sets of 40.

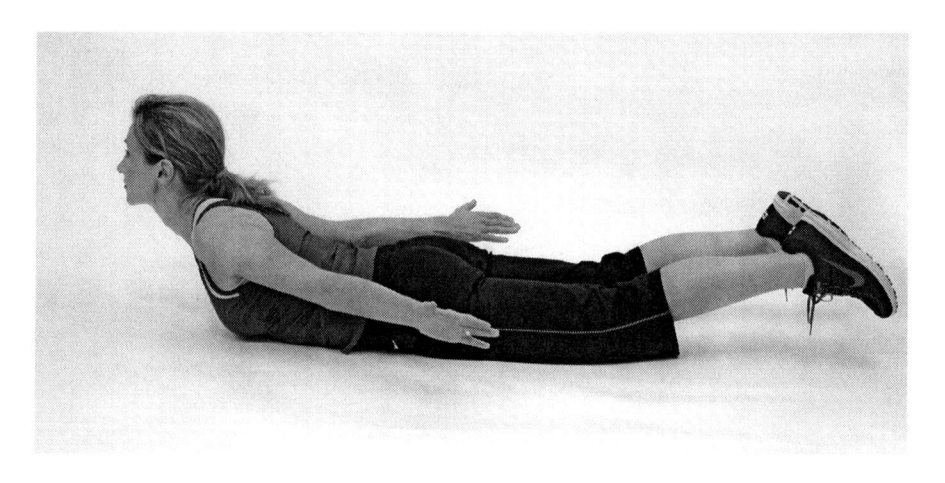

GENERAL POSTURE IMPROVEMENT

EXERCISE 13: Abs Stretch

Starting Position: On the floor, legs flat underneath and holding yourself with your arms.

Exercise: Push up with your arms and look up and back, feeling the stretch in your abdominal area. Hold the stretch for a count of at least 10. Remember to breathe.

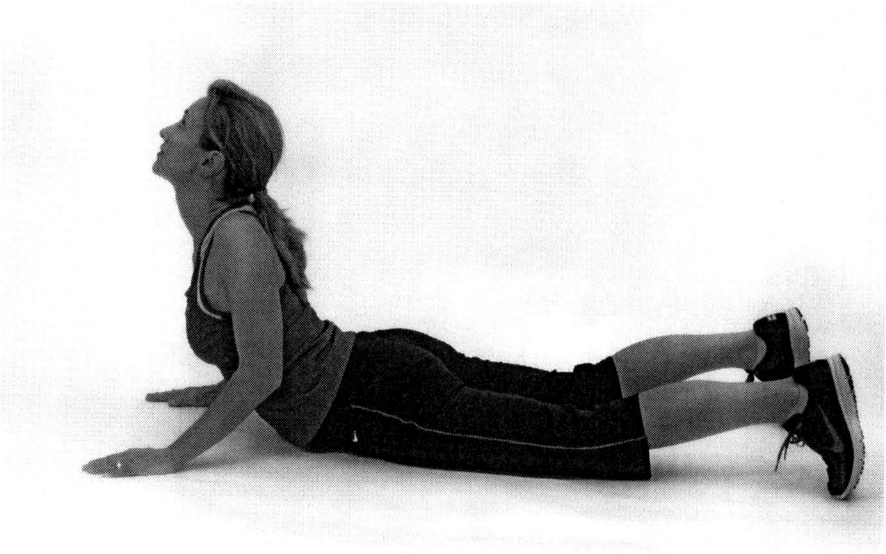

EXERCISES FOR IMPROVING FORWARD HEAD POSTURE, ROUNDED SHOULDERS, AND THE "HUMP"

IMPROVING NECK & SHOULDER POSTURE

EXERCISE 1: Stretching the neck

Starting Position: Start with your head in a neutral position, looking straight ahead.

Exercise: Tilt you chin up and contract the back of the neck muscles to form an arch in the neck. Your chin should be tilted about 30 degrees. Return to neutral position. Repeat five times.

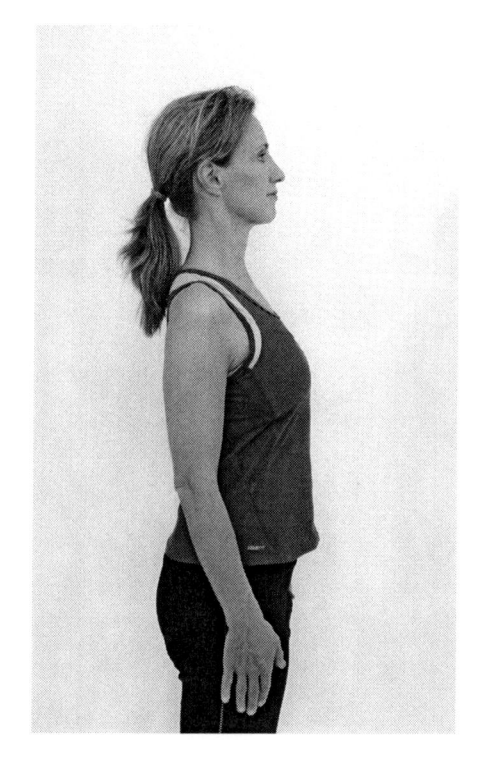

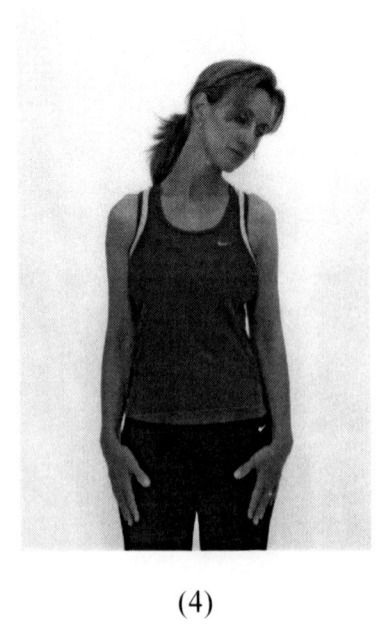

150 *Posture Confidence: Everything You Need To Change Your Posture For Good*

(2)

(3)

(4)

IMPROVING NECK & SHOULDER POSTURE

EXERCISE 2: Shoulders

Start in a standing position with your arms at your side. Roll your shoulders forward, down, back, and then up. Repeat 3 times.

Then reverse the order, roll your shoulders forward, up, back and down. Repeat 3 times.

Always end with the shoulder rolls back. You want to give your shoulders lots of opportunity to be pulled back and stay that way.

(1)

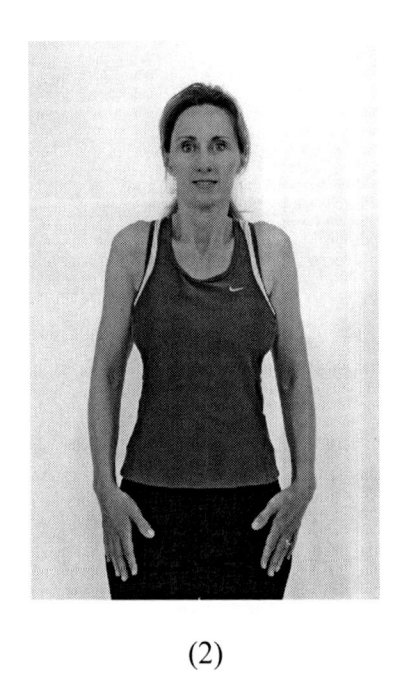

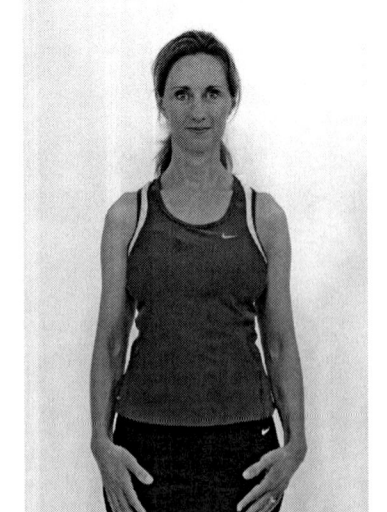

(2)

(3)

(4)

IMPROVING NECK & SHOULDER POSTURE

EXERCISE 3: Shoulders

Starting Position: Stand with arms extended and elbows slightly bent.

Exercise: Roll shoulders forward and swing arms in big circles. Repeat 3 times. Reverse the circles and go the other direction. Repeat 3 times. Three times forward and three times back equal 1 set. Perform 3 sets.

IMPROVING NECK & SHOULDER POSTURE

EXERCISE 4: Shoulders

Starting Position: Stand with arms extended in front of you.

Exercise: Bring both arms over your head and stretch long and tall. Hold it there while you breathe in deeply. Now exhale. Bring your arms back down and shake your arms out. Repeat 3 times.

IMPROVING NECK & SHOULDER POSTURE

EXERCISE 5: Trapezius

Starting Position: Draw up your shoulders as close to your ears as possible, contracting your trapezius muscles.

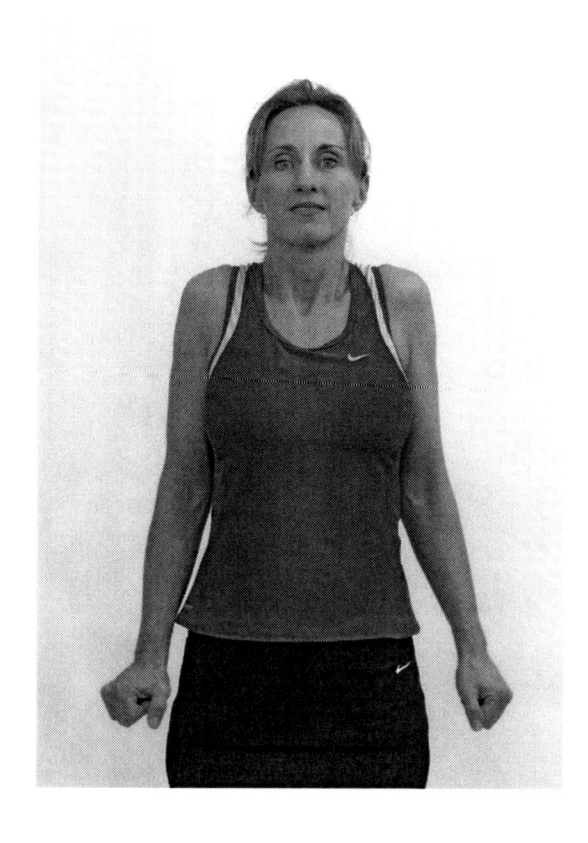

Exercise: Pull shoulders down as far as you can to help stretch and elongate this muscle.

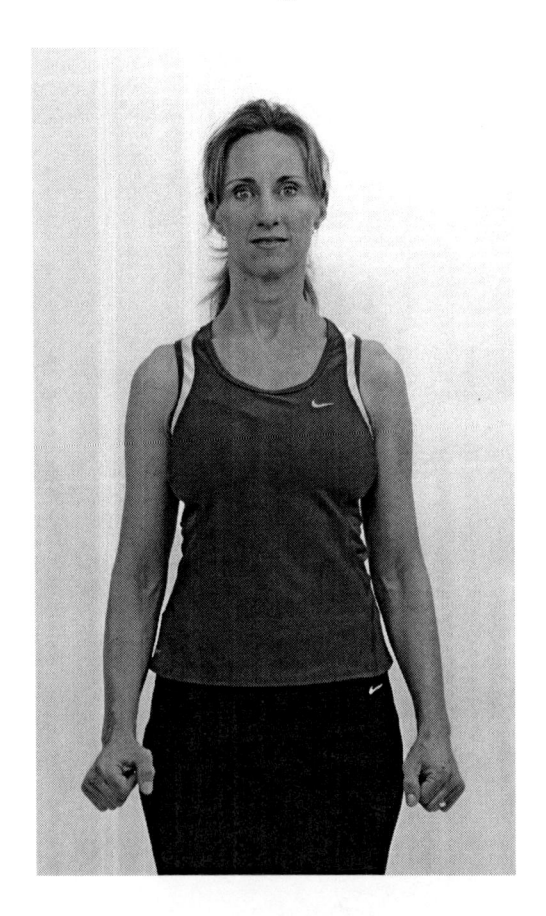

IMPROVING NECK & SHOULDER POSTURE

EXERCISE 6: Latissmus Dorsi

Starting Position: Arms out to your side, full extending your arms with your elbows bent. Arms should be slightly above your shoulders.

Exercise: Focus on bringing your shoulder blades down and into the spine. Bring your elbows down, squeezing hard and moving them slightly behind your body. Hold for a count of "1" and return to the starting position. 3 sets of 15, use light weight.

Starting Position: Rear View

Exercise: Rear View

IMPROVING NECK & SHOULDER POSTURE

EXERCISE 7: Neck

Starting Position: Start with your head in a neutral position looking forward.

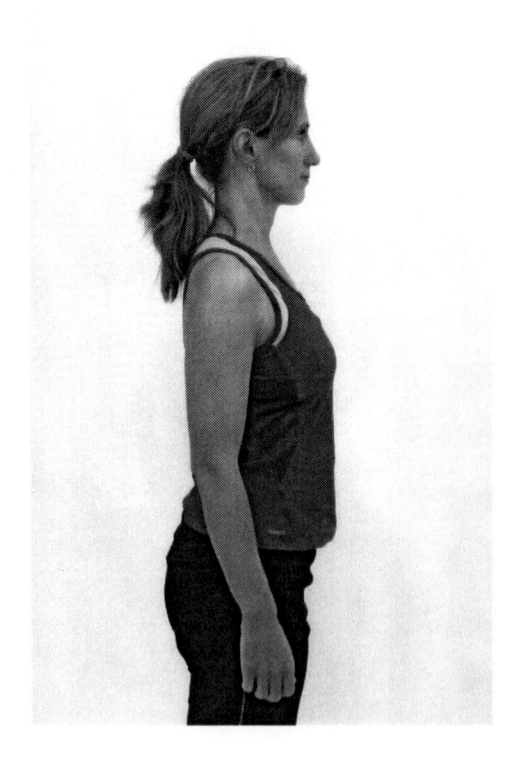

Exercise: Contract the muscles in the back of your neck to bring your neck straight back. Keep you head from tilting in any direction. This exercise will help to lead your muscles just below the base of your skull. Repeat 5 times.

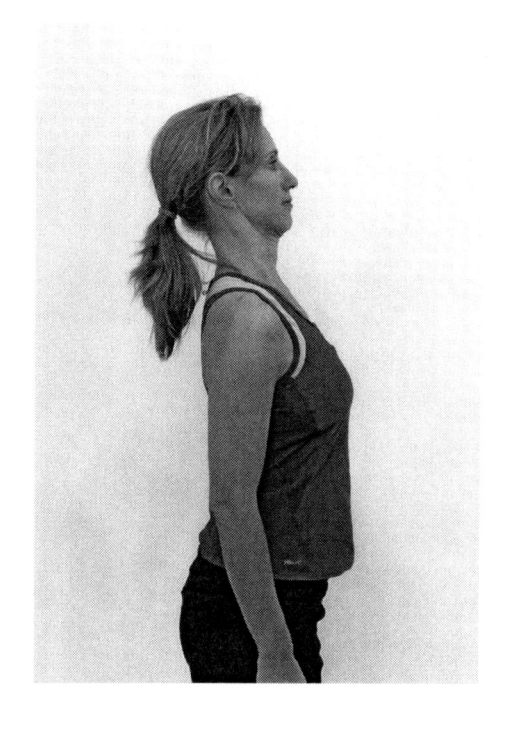

Exercise: Contract the muscles in the back of your neck to bring your neck straight back. Use your hand to apply gentle pressure to your chin at the end point (once you've brought your head back as far as you can). Pressure should be slight and should not produce pain. Stop if painful. Repeat 5 times.

IMPROVING NECK & SHOULDER POSTURE

EXERCISE 8: Pectoralis

Starting Position: Find a doorway. The drawback here is that the doorway is a fixed size. The size may or may not be ideal for you. Remember to do both sides.

Exercise:

1. <u>Inferior Pecs</u>: Raise hand to where shoulder is almost fully extended. Again elbow is still supported by the wall. Lean forward. Stretch out the lower part of the pectoralis. (*You are also stretching your latissmus.*) Hold for a count of "20."

2. <u>Middle Pecs</u>: Hand and elbow should contact the door frame. Lean forward and stretch out the pectoralis muscles for a count of "20."

3. <u>Superior Pecs:</u> Lower arm to where hand is level with your shoulder. Elbow is almost bent completely. Lean forward. Focus on stretching the top part of your pectoralis. Hold for a count of "20."

166 *Posture Confidence: Everything You Need To Change Your Posture For Good*

(1)

(2)

(3)

IMPROVING NECK & SHOULDER POSTURE

EXERCISE 9: Rhomboids

Starting Position: Arms out to your side, full extending your arms with your elbows bent.

Exercise: Focus on bringing your shoulder blades together and slightly down. This movement will naturally cause your arms to go back 2 to 3 inches. Hold for a count of "1" and return to the starting position. 3 sets of 15.

Starting Position: Side View

Exercise: Side View

IMPROVING NECK & SHOULDER POSTURE

EXERCISE 10: Teres Minor

Starting Position: Stand straight with your back and abdominals tight. Shoulder blades are pulled back and down. Arms are down at your side with your elbows bent at 90 degrees.

Exercise: Rotate your arms away from your midline, keeping your elbows at your side. Contract the muscles that draw your arm back and squeeze. 3 sets of 15, use light weight.

Starting Position: Side View

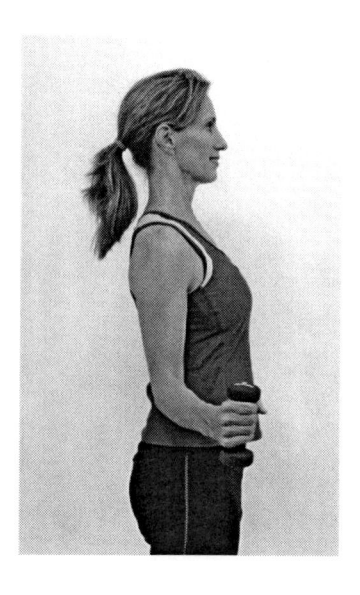

Exercise: Side View

ADDITIONAL INFORMATION:

Still have questions? Want to share a testimonial?

Posture Confidence

1770 Saint James Place # 210
Houston, TX 77056
support@postureconfidence.com

Visit our websites! Order the DVDs!

Posture Confidence
http://www.postureconfidence.com

Improve My Posture
http://www.improvemyposture.com

Stop Computer Posture
http://www.stopcomputerposture.com

Better Posture For Kids
http://www.betterpostureforkids.com